**April Kirkwood** is a Licensed Professional Counselor with two masters degrees (school and community counseling) in education. April has spent more than 25 years in public education and in the mental health field as a social worker, teacher, guidance counselor, and mentor for new teachers. She presently works as a mental health counselor. Her specialties include women's mental health issues focusing on early childhood trauma as well as molestation, divorce, co-dependence, and addiction. April also spends time as a public speaker and facilitator of workshops. April's professional focus is on the transformation from #MeToo into #NowME, a process which helps patients heal and rebuild their lives. Telling her story is another way for April to help others with their own stories and challenges. www.aprilkirkwood.com

**Donald G. Evans** is the Founding Executive Editor of the Chicago Literary Hall of Fame, author of the novel *Good Money After Bad*, and editor of a Chicago Cubs anthology *Cubbie Blues: 100 Years of Waiting Till Next Year*. His short story collection, *An Off-White Christmas*, will be published in October, 2018. He's been listed four times in the *Newcity* Lit 50: Who Really Books in Chicago feature, and received the Chicago Writers Association's Spirit Award for lifetime achievement. He serves on various boards and committees, including as a program committee member of the American Writers Museum, and a selector for the annual Harold Washington Literary Award. www.donaldgevans.com

# SUMMARY

For rural Ohio beauty queen April Kirkwood, her #MeToo moment came way before the term was coined. She lost her virginity to the middle-aged Frankie Valli at 16, after a decade pursuing a childhood fantasy to be the crooner's wife. The affair would go on (and off, and on) for decades.

But Frankie Valli is just a central character in April's complex story of her struggle to break the generational cycle of abused and dependent women. Indeed, the strong women in *Working My Way Back to Me* are filled with enormous love that offers protection, but also intensifies the hurt. Through April's eyes, we experience joys and heartaches that echo across more than a half-century of old family secrets and ways, and the triumphs and defeats involved in trying to break the mold.

April Lynn Kirkwood was not yet six years old when she first met Frankie Valli at a concert in Youngstown, Ohio, known as Bomb Town, USA, in part because of its reputation for Mafia influence. From there, April weaves a story of her ever-growing obsession with the pop star, and how her female relatives aided and abetted her seemingly preposterous quest. From a young age, against the backdrop of violence and abuse and molestation at home, April was the family's salvation. Their future star. Their Somebody, Someday. Sweet little April sang and danced to *Four Seasons* tunes, as she amassed a collection of Frankie Valli memorabilia. Schoolgirl April strived to master the baton and dance, while using her Barbie and Ken dolls to create an intricate light and love-filled future for her and the celebrity singer. Adolescent April cultivated grace and manners, all the time hoping to become the kind of girl to whom Frankie would one day be devoted. Almost-Grown Up April won over pageant judges, keeping in mind Frankie's advice to always stay beautiful. Young Adult April clung to her love for Frankie, simultaneously failing at relationships with a string of Frankie prototypes. April, all through the years, with the tacit approval of a mother desperate to raise a star, pursued her idol from concert to concert, dressed in her straw Frankie hat and Frankie sash.

April's eccentric cast of characters includes a born-again grandmother, a pill-popping seductress mother, a child molester grandfather, a bruiser father in-law, a timid father, a riotous aunt, an upper-crust degenerate gambler, a funk musician, and many others.

***Working My Way Back to Me*** is an inspirational tale that sheds light on universal struggles involving love, sexuality, addiction, and mental health. April's adventures lead to betrayal and suffering, and her fate depends, in part, on her female relatives' ability to protect and empower a better future. April must learn the fine line between guidance and sabotage as she claws her way to a future not as a savior, but as her own fiercely accomplished woman.

# WORKING MY WAY BACK TO ME

*A Frank Memoir of Self-Discovery*

## By April Kirkwood

### (with DG Evans)

Boudoir Press
Stuart, Florida

To Dana and Grant--my children, my teachers, my life. Thanks for your unconditional love, your frankness, and your ability to correct and encourage all at once. Thanks most of all for choosing me to be your mom.

# PREFACE

By April Kirkwood

Frankie Valli happened, for me, a long time ago. But distance did not help me cure the damage I'd incurred in this relationship, nor did it allow me to process all the whos, whats, wheres, whens, whys, and hows. I started writing. My first attempt was a kind of cleansing, in which I furiously recorded feelings and events, events and feelings. I put to paper every random notion I had about love, sex, relationships, family, life—in no particular order. It felt important, in that initial rush of energy, to yell to the world whatever came into my head.

This, most experienced writers know, is the essence of a first draft. You get thoughts down, develop the story, and try to get it whole; then the real work starts. I am not an experienced writer. In lieu of revision, I rushed that first draft into print, not really knowing that so much of the real difficult work lay ahead. I sold a handful of copies, did some radio and print interviews, and generally treated the experience as a coming out party for my story.

What I'd published, then, was tantamount to a diary. I gave readers a peak at my private thoughts, but without much context or clarity. It was like, "Here." The book then was called *Big Girls Do Cry*, and it was forgotten almost immediately, like a self-erasing tape.

Four years later, I felt ready to finally and truly conquer that story. I wanted it to make sense for readers, but first it had to make sense to me. I was getting closer to some kind of understanding about what that was, and how the person in that memoir turned into the person I am today. It helped that I'd found a truly remarkable woman, Val Gobos, who believed in my story. She wanted to see the story get attention, find readers and viewers, and generally be a vehicle for not only my own healing but that of other women. Val thought I needed to enlist a professional writer to help me revise and edit the original manuscript. Don Evans was that writer.

The first thing Don told me was, "This is not a book about Frankie Valli; it's a book about April Kirkwood." Soon, we'd trashed almost the entire first book (or, as Don says, "used it for parts") and started a process that involved interviews between us; targeted writing exercises in which I was made to explore the uncomfortable truths of that time; drafting and redrafting. I learned how to extract the truth from myself, and how to turn that truth into story. Don made me focus on characters and scenes. He demanded, over and over, for me to figure out the details and connections. He insisted I dig harder.

That I tell the truth.

The result is that, unlike the first book, I was able to conjure the world I inhabited when I was five, ten, sixteen, twenty. I was able to put together the various pieces of the jigsaw puzzle in a way that made a vivid picture. I was able to seize those long-ago moments, hold them in my hand, and share them. And when I turned the serious writing over to Don, he made the words sing, the images pop, and the laughter ring.

Along the way, there were tears, sobs, heaving. I'll admit: I was not okay. The writing process, though, made me confront all of my fears and failures. It made me take personal responsibility for my actions. It also helped me to see the intricate web of influences that helped push me places I should never have gone. And it made me better equipped to hear the stories of so many other women who, like me, are damaged, but not beyond repair.

So now I'm releasing my story again. This time I feel like I don't need to shout to be heard.

# CONTENTS

# MEETING FRANKIE

Mine was a pink-and-white world. At least on the surface. My bedspreads and canopy were pink and white; my favorite dress and shoes were pink and white; my French provincial lamp was pink and white; even my pj's, slippers, and robe were pink and white. My bedroom in the little converted upstairs apartment, with its high, pointed ceiling, looked like a chapel, and through the cross-shaped bars of my octagonal window, I looked out on a stand of pine trees fronting the wide-open fields of rural Liberty, Ohio. Our side of the street had six houses, but there were none yet on the other side, and that open plain represented unlimited possibilities to my five-year-old imagination.

The clangs and bashes coming from Mom and Les's next-door bedroom were hardly pink and white, though: more like blue and black. Mom and Les knocked each other all over the house. Les would kick Mom down the stairs—kick, kick, kick, fall—and she would tear at his hair—rip, rip, rip—and they would both scream, scream, scream. Mom's were all-weather sunglasses.

I balanced a book on my head as I tiptoed from one side of my teeny room to the other. Posture was important, and grace. *Stand with shoulders back*, Mom would say. *Your smile is important. You need to stay thin.* We'd moved into this apartment a year earlier, after Mom and Les had made things official, and though I cried to leave Grandma Kata's house, we were still only a mile away. My safe place was just one light over and across.

My little white poodle, Ricky Lynn, wagged his tail, shook his pink collar, and watched my slow pacing. Ricky Lynn came to me as a bribe, the price for my acquiescence in a move I hated with all my heart, a sort of "Stop Crying and Pet Your Dog" payoff. The poodle got my middle name, as would my brother some years down the road, and while Ricky Lynn sounded like a country music singer and looked like a beauty-schooled albino rat, he was mine, all mine, and I loved him with everything I had.

Les hated Ricky Lynn from Day 1: too much yapping, too many messes, too much responsibility. Les thought Ricky Lynn lacked proper respect for his authority, and meant to cower him in an old-school, Out-To-The-Woodshed kind of way. "God-damned DOG!," he'd yell, face beet red, barreled chest inflated, fists clenched. Les's intense blue eyes took on a frightening sheen against the backdrop of the navy police uniform that had first seduced Mom. His hulking frame, his raised voice, his sudden outbursts, that sidearm you never really noticed or stopped noticing… it all foreshadowed some kind of doom. I silently accepted my role as Ricky Lynn's protector.

Soon, Aunt Ginny and Lydia would arrive to take me to my very first concert: Frankie Valli and the Four Seasons at Stambaugh Auditorium in Youngstown.

This was 1963, and music was already a big part of my life, or at least big in five-year-old terms. I played Nancy Sinatra's "These Boots Are Made For Walkin'" and Leslie Gore's "It's My Party" over and over on my pink-and-white portable record player. More often, I listened to the *Bye Bye Birdie* soundtrack and mimicked Ann-Margret's wild dance moves. Saturdays, if we got the house cleaned, we'd be allowed to eat our out-of-the-can chicken noodle soup, and dip our buttered crackers in front of *American Bandstand* on the gargantuan console in Grandma Kata's piano room.

The bells from Cedars Corner First Presbyterian Church gonged, and I knew it was almost time. On cue, Aunt Ginny pulled up to the curb in her blue '61 Chevy. I ran downstairs in my dress with leotards and black patent leather shoes, a red coat with white muff, and earmuffs. I hopped into the backseat. (This was *way* before car seats or even the regular use of seatbelts.) We drove.

This was fall, and like everything in my childhood memories, beautiful. We zoomed past the little convenience store at the bottom of my street, the place where we got our Isaly's Chipped Chopped Ham. We saw the blur of Webb's ice cream shop, closed for the season. Eventually, a little plaza with a dry cleaner, hair stylist, and grocery store would muscle its way into this country corner, but then, just then, my world was simple—unadorned, uncluttered, untouched.

We were excited. Aunt Ginny was excited; Ginny's friend Lydia was excited; I was excited. Aunt Ginny took me everywhere. She was 11 years older, so we weren't exactly peers, but she wasn't my babysitter, either. More, we liked being together, like friends. That was how I thought of it, anyway. As often as not, I called her Gigi, which was not only an affectionate nickname but also my way of showing we were on equal terms. Besides, everybody thought it was better for me to hang out with my teenaged aunt and her teenaged friends than to be around the violence at home. But this—going to a live music concert to see a popular singer and his band—*this* was special.

Stambaugh was and is an Ohio institution, as much known for proms, wedding receptions, and reunions as for concerts. It was a stately old marble building that I recognized immediately.

This was where we started going to church after Mom married Les and took me away from Grandma Kata's farm. The famous Evangelical healer Kathryn Kuhlman made regular visits to Stambaugh, and I remember, as part of the youth group, that I was not allowed to sit until I'd gone under her power. We spoke in tongues. People fainted and had revelations. Les ushered. Mom sobbed. On the way to Stambaugh, there was the usual fighting, but on the way home we always went to Perkins for pancakes.

Stambaugh held two thousand people, maybe a bit more, but at five years old, it seemed unimaginably large. We found our seats, and it seemed like all the world paused, waiting, when the house lights went down, and the bright lights powed the stage. I didn't know Frankie Valli and the Four Seasons yet, but this was during their ascent in popularity. Just in the last year or so, they'd had hit singles with "Sherry," "Big Girls Don't Cry," "Walk Like A Man," and others. They'd played "Sherry" on *American Bandstand* the previous year.

The run-up to the show seemed agonizingly long. Then: there he was. The crazed shrieks and cries, the long ovation, all of it went away, and as I stared up at this tiny Italian man—gorgeous in his impeccable outfit and black hair—I swear I was staring at my father, my real father, the failed clothes salesman who I visited every other week in Grandma Gatta's basement in Niles. The semi-professional sax man who played weddings and fairs, and who serenaded me with "Moon River." The man who said he loved me only later, after I won a beauty contest.

I was mesmerized. Once the band twanged to life and Frankie started singing, I recognized some of the songs, the melodies. There were originals and covers, a sort of blend of doo-wop and pop featuring Frankie's gorgeous falsetto voice. The music was intensely emotional and yet fun. I couldn't stop staring at the lead singer. Everything they played was a crowd pleaser.

The whole concert was a sweaty, pulsating dream, a surreal experience that at once seemed to last forever and end in a blink.

It had never occurred to me that I'd feel the music—I mean, literally *feel* the music—vibrating through my body. When it was over, Frankie Valli came into the audience. He walked right into us, into *me*, and then he signed my concert program. He signed *my… concert… program!* I blushed, a pink-and-white blush.

Later, as Mom tucked me into bed, I rattled on about my night, delirious about the concert and amazed at my meeting with Frankie Valli. Mom shushed me, then dropped to her knees. She closed her eyes and chanted, "Now I lay me down to sleep, I pray the Lord my soul to keep, guard me Jesus, through the night, and wake me to the morning light." Then she added, "God Bless April, God Bless Aunt Ginny. And God Bless Frankie."

This, for me, was the beginning, not the end, of… something.

*April rides her tricycle at Grandma Kata's farm in Liberty Township, circa 1961.*

# CHASING FRANKIE

I roused myself from bed the following morning, lifeless from the rare late night out, and yet peppy, inspired, *alive*!

Mom, as always, had plopped down on our little blue kitchen table a box of Frosted Flakes with Tony the Tiger smiling at me, and when I came to breakfast she poured cereal and milk into my bowl, gazing at the mail and the box top prize advertisements. She poured me a cup of hot tea, into which I snuck spoonful after spoonful of sugar, while she sipped her instant coffee. Ricky Lynn, groggy, too, from our late night, dutifully shimmied against my leg, begging for scraps. He wagged his tail.

"Arp, arp," he said.

"Good little boy," I cooed, using my tiniest, squeakiest voice.

I plucked a Frosted Flake from the bowl, cupped it in my hand, and discreetly held it out for Ricky Lynn. He slurped it up and then licked my hand, little kisses of gratitude. I patted his head and looked over toward the staircase, knowing that if Les appeared I'd have to move fast to get Ricky Lynn to the safety of my bedroom.

I sat with my concert program laid out before me, eating distractedly, all thoughts trained on Frankie Valli. The concert program showed pictures of the Four Seasons in Akron and Cleveland, shots of the band dressed in v-neck sweaters, tuxedos, shimmering suits. In some, Frankie's narrow tie and pressed white shirt indicated a kind of Boy-Next-Door charm; in others, his dangling necklace hinted at a more street savvy Guy-On-The-Corner mystique. In photo after photo, he stood front and center. The program was an homage to Frankie: his words, his smile, his charm, his achievements. In my program, and now in my head, Frankie Valli was everything. I was obsessing not so much about what I'd just experienced but about how to get more.

There was a happiness about me, I remember that. Here I was, just a nice little farm girl, too young for romantic love—puberty still far off, in the *way* distant future—too poor for celebrity hobnobbing, a girl accustomed to catnapping in a church pew and collecting chicken eggs. But in our small, rural town, I was not too young to know about boys and girls, men and women. I had the chalk outline of the way adult relationships happened, at least enough to know that they happened one way in fairy tales and very differently at home. And I definitely wanted Fairy Tale Love, not Mom-Les Love.

"Mom," I asked, sweetly. "Can I get a Frankie Valli album?"

I looked over at Mom. Her toast sat cold on a plate, and her head was buried in a dishrag, from where a faint sob escaped. Weekends at home, there were always arguments, often loud, shrieking exchanges from behind Les and Mom's closed bedroom door. Crying came later, little jagged moans and aches that popped out of Mom while she was puttering around the house, or when we were shopping, or just in spare moments of solitude.

Mom was known as Queen Bee, not always in a kind way. She looked like Princess Grace with her piercing green-blue eyes and short bobbed hair layered upon her head. Her skin was the purest white, and those eyes against that ivory backdrop emitted an aura of vivaciousness and, though I didn't think of it that way at the time, sex. Mom used her sex appeal to get her way, or tried to, anyway. Women throughout the greater Youngstown area—moms from school, neighbors, co-workers—hated, *hated* Mom. But men loved her. Mom was the most gorgeous and messed up person in my whole family, which was saying something. She had affairs with Dean Borden and Bill Somebody from Packard Electric. She had an affair with her psychiatrist, Ralph Walton, and probably Dr. Harry Davis, a gorgeous farm doctor from Vienna with whom Grandma Kata also had messed around. Grandma Kata's former boyfriend, Paul Galetti, the father of my Aunt Lerene, was in love with Mom. Paul was a supervisor of some sort at Packard Electric, and it was he who got Mom and Aunt Ginny their jobs. These were married men, every one of them.

Two white pills sat on the napkin next to Mom's coffee cup. She picked up the mug with one hand, blew on the coffee, then picked up the pills with the other hand. She popped the pills into her mouth, swagged her head back, and washed them down with a big gulp. This was the era of Mommy's Little Helpers. That's how my mom kick-started her days.

"Sure, Peanut," Mom said. "Of course."

"And, Mom?"

"Yes?"

"Can we go see Frankie Valli again?"

Frankie's autograph—already, I was thinking of him as *Frankie*—was a beautiful, fun Humpty Dumpty scrawl. The little "F" outside an egg-shaped loop looked like a clothespin jumping rope; indecipherable little squiggles made a runway; another big loop slowed the pace; then a crazy concoction of Etch-a-Sketch shapes and waves crashed to a big finish.

And so began my pursuit.

My first Frankie Valli album was *Sherry and 11 Others*, a

black-and-white cover in which Frankie and the Seasons wore pink polo shirts over white t-shirts. The title track popped yellow. I played it over and over, sometimes moving the needle back to "Sherry" or "Big Girls Don't Cry" over and over when the songs ended, until the vinyl wore bare, and until Mom got me *Big Girls Don't Cry and Twelve Others,* with Frankie and the band sporting impeccable double-breasted navy suits, stringy ties, and short hair. In both albums, the band was set in a circle. Through the long, cold Ohio winter, I listened and I sang and I plotted.

There was my real life and there was my imaginary life, and the two would often overlap. My Fashion Queen Barbie doll, with three wigs, became April, and my Ken Doll, whose blonde hair I magic marker-ed black, became Frankie. I changed April's wigs to suit the occasion, and outfitted Ken in a Frankie-esque black suit and plastic black shoes that caused me severe panic when they inevitably got misplaced. If the doll wasn't dressed right, it wasn't Frankie. I was a spoiled only child who got basically everything she wanted, and what I wanted were accessories. I got a blue Barbie convertible, then a house, a garden, a pool, then a dog, finally a baby and a baby bottle. I was making a life for these two, April and Frankie. At home, April and Frankie and their ever-expanding universe eventually took up all the floor space in my bedroom, such that nobody could walk into my room. When I went to Dad's house for visitation, or Grandma Kata's, I brought it all along in a carrying case. In my fantasy play, April and Frankie drove around town together. We waved at our admirers. We bought a house together and furnished it. We made a baby and loved it to death. When Frankie went to his concerts, April either tagged along or kissed him good-bye. Both April and Frankie dressed stylishly, as befitted their charmed lives. My girlfriends collected dolls—the various Barbie Ponytail dolls, the Barbie Swirl Ponytail, the Barbie Bubblecut dolls, and later the Miss Barbie, American Girl Barbie, and Color Magic Barbie—but I insisted on just the one. I was loyal to April, and to

Frankie.

In 1964 it was not easy to stalk. Our only real news sources were the *Youngstown Vindicator* and the weekly *Liberty News*. Like a lot of rags, these papers focused on news and events centered on our hometown. Meaning that a Four Seasons concert in Pittsburgh or Cincinnati or Ann Arbor or anywhere else did not warrant a mention. At five and then six-years old, and with no obvious tracking skills, I needed co-conspirators. In Mom, Grandma Kata, and Aunt Ginny, I had them.

The following spring, we began a weekly ritual of driving to Girard, Ohio, to an old-fashioned newspaper/cigar store on a little corner of State Street. These were adventures—me and Aunt Ginny and Grandma Kata, full of hope, anticipation, the thrill of the chase. We were united in one goal: find Frankie!

It was only a ten-minute drive to Girard, but it had all the markings of a road trip. In our simple lives, this passed for adventure, and we were caught up in that spirit. We passed Blackstone Funeral Parlor over the hill, where everybody in our family got buried. We blew past Shannon Road and sometimes detoured past the First Christian Assembly, with all its Holy Rollers. We passed the sites where the annual carnival and Independence Day parades took place.

Grandma Kata slipped us a few dollars and stayed in the car while Aunt Ginny and I went hunting. Cigar smoke wafted from the back room; newspapers and magazines hung on racks and were stacked on the glass counter; the ornate brass cash register went ca-ching ca-ching as customers came and went with their smokes, their gum, the newspapers, their breath mints.

Aunt Ginny did the heavy lifting. She'd scour the classifieds and coming events, the news in a dozen different papers throughout Ohio, Michigan, Indiana, Pennsylvania, even New York. Her beehive hairdo towered above the racks as she licked the tips of her beautiful, gentle hands to flip pages. She wore open-toed shoes that showed off her lovely feet, and dark glasses that perched on her slender, beak-like nose. We didn't know where notice of an upcoming Frankie Valli concert might be tucked, and so Aunt Ginny's eyes raced over even obscure items on the off chance the lead might be buried.

The first trip, we came up empty, and then again, and again, each time hauling off a half-dozen newspapers to continue our search back home. We'd spread the papers over the floor. Ginny would study the fine print. I'd make funny page imprints with my Silly Putty. Ricky Lynn would grab a corner and shake the newspaper in his mouth.

But every weekend throughout that spring, we'd pile back into the car and make our trek to Girard, each time enjoying the trip, and each time convincing ourselves this time we'd hit pay dirt. Finally, in May, we stumbled across an announcement in the Toledo paper: Frankie Valli and the Four Seasons were scheduled to play later that summer at Cedar Point Amusement Park in Sandusky, Ohio.

We cheered, we screamed. We were old lottery players whose numbers had just come up. Grandma Kata smiled, and clarified the ground rules. This would be my "summer event," the sunny special day that appeared, occasionally, between all the other gray days. "Not every day is supposed to be sunny," Grandma Kata said. "But that one sunny day carries you through all the gray days until you get to another sunny day."

Grandma Kata, not yet 50 then, seemed impossibly old. She was solid, with muscular arms and shoulders, and a tank-like frame. Her big bosoms formed a mountain pressing out against conservative clothes. She was often serious. She was a doer. Now, she twinkled a little smile, and it felt not as though that sunny day was coming but that it was already here. I was going to see Frankie Valli again, and I did not intend to squander the opportunity.

*April cradles her doll in Grandma's Kata's front yard.*

# DEAD LITTLE DOG

Ricky Lynn had escaped. I knew I hadn't left the backdoor open, and Mom swore she hadn't, either. "God-*damn* that dog!" Les screamed.

Those early years of my obsession with Frankie Valli were sweet. In retrospect, I wanted a man to love and protect and adore me. My own father, shy and awkward and removed, hardly figured into my life. Instead, I had Les. Big, mean, impulsive, angry, leering Les. He made me afraid. He *wanted* me afraid.

"We have to find Ricky Lynn!" I screeched. I started to cry. Ricky Lynn was an indoor dog, and while we occasionally let him out, it was always under close supervision. Now, I could not be sure how long he'd been gone, how far he had roamed.

"I HATE that god-*damned* dog!!!" Les yelled.

"We'll find him, honey," Mom said, softly. "We just have to look."

Mom's body turned from Les, who was now rampaging

through the house, kicking under the sofa, whapping the garbage can to the floor. Mom's body language said she was at once ready to run and ready to fight. I hustled upstairs to my room.

I was panicked. Les was put out. He bellowed a series of profanities as he punished the house, and I knew instinctively that it behooved me to find Ricky Lynn before Les did. I slumped down on the floor of my room, paralyzed, sobbing. "Come on, April," Mom urged from the bottom of the stairs.

Frankie's "I Can't Give You Anything But Love" had been playing on my turntable, but the song had reached its conclusion. I heard the click as the arm lifted and then glided back to rest. Funny how I could make any Frankie song about anything. In that moment, the lyrics spoke directly to my relationship with Ricky Lynn, my role as his mother, the one person in the world who loved him unconditionally and would not let anything hurt him.

We were now a search party, all of us calling, "Ricky Lynn! Come on, boy!" Mom and I scoured the yard. Mr. and Mrs. Habor, our landlords, heard the commotion and took off down the block, looking. Les raced out to the driveway, keys in hand. I heard the engine roar to life.

Our search of the yard proved fruitless. In my head, Ricky Lynn would never deliberately leave. I gave him all my love, and made it my mission to grant him a happy life. Rather than running loose, it was more likely he was cowering in a closet, or way back under a bed. I sprinted back upstairs to my room, knowing that was where Ricky Lynn would always return.

That was when I heard the terrifying screech of brakes, the helpless whimper, the Habors' startled cries. I heard the car door slam. Angry bickering between Mom and Les. I sprinted downstairs, where Mom met me at the door. "I don't want you to see this, April," she insisted. Mom urged me back upstairs and lay down on the bed with me.

I can't remember when I stopped screaming, stopped crying.

Mom's arms were around me, but I never felt so helpless. So alone. Eventually, I dove into a deep slumber. Les would claim it was all an accident, and we knew better than to disagree. Besides, what good would it do? Ricky Lynn, my precious little dog, was dead, and with him a small part of me. I remember, in the days that followed, my sorrow turning to resolve. Resolve to do what, or how: none of that was clear.

*Les and Mom going to church at Stambaugh Auditorium.*

# CUTE LITTLE ME!

We started driving in a pre-dawn darkness that followed a sleepless night. The smell of baloney sandwiches and pretzels escaped Grandma Kata's packed lunch sacks. We rattled and hummed our way toward light, Aunt Ginny turning the radio knob, me, huddled under a blanket, asking, "Are we almost there yet?" It was three hours to Sandusky, and although we were drowsy, we were excited, too. We had plans, plans to review, refine, replenish. Mom, of course, had bowed out, merely saying, "Not going."

The Cedar Point Amusement Park entrance gate was open at 10 a.m. and already long lines had formed. Throngs of families waited to get inside. The parking lot was bigger than any I'd ever seen, so big we had to write down our row and number so we could find the car later. The smell of cotton candy and caramel apples sweetened the air, and at every turn, flowers and fountains lent pageantry to an almost dreamlike atmosphere. The various sounds blended into a kind of music: the rumble of the Blue

Streak roller coaster on its frightening ascent, then the crescendo of screams as it tumbled downward; the unmistakable pitch of the Rotor Ride as it reached peak velocity just before the bottom fell out of the barrel; the rhythmic splish splashes of the Wave Pool. Tchaikovsky for children.

But we weren't there to ride the rides or munch the treats or smell the roses. Our job was to see Frankie Valli.

Our mission had begun months before, and Mom, Grandma Kata, and Aunt Ginny—three powerhouse women—were dead set on making this happen. The Cedar Point concert had been our North Star, helping us find our way into the future, into now.

"If you want to meet a star, act like you know what you're doing," Grandma Kata had said.

"Just go in, put your head up in the air," Mom had added.

Everybody in the family had advice like that, home remedies for how to court royalty, and me, church-going little budding beauty queen that I was, would not think to ask, "How would *you* know?"

"I want him to point at me when he sings," I declared.

Standing between Grandma Kata and Aunt Ginny, the heat of the day just tippling toward its peak, I felt secure and confident and special. I was dressed for the show. A white silk pageant banner reading "FRANKIE" in all capitals lay draped across my shoulders. My faux straw hat, made of plastic, had "FRANKIE" glittered across it in purple, where previously the name of some politician or another had been. My gold sandals set off the whole sparkly outfit. I'd essentially gift-wrapped myself for Frankie Valli.

"Three, please," Grandma Kata said.

We'd been working months to get to this day—picking up fabric and ribbon and glitter and other craft materials at five-and-dime stores and yard sales. This work was a welcome distraction from what was happening at home. I'd grown ever-more homesick for Grandma Kata's farm, and had begun, increasingly, to hate our apartment. Weird kaleidoscopic colors emanated from my stop sign-shaped stained glass window. Stuffy, stale air permeated my room, and the outside fresh air seemed unobtainable, far. Cracks and pows and bangs filtered through the thin wall separating my room from Mom and Les's room. I wouldn't even drink the water; I wanted only Grandma Kata's water. I associated our apartment with the ruckus of Mom and Les hurting each other, hanging onto each other, making loud accusations—him, then her, punch, counter punch—hitting, fleeing, both of them at once suspects and detectives, rubber-gloving the cold clues of their lives. Above it all hung the ghost of poor little Ricky Lynn.

Grandma Kata's farm, on the other hand, was all tranquility and love, simple pleasures that couldn't be penetrated by harsh realities. There wasn't much money, but that feeling never touched us kids. Grandpa—Bumpy, we called him—worked in the Sheet and Tube mill, while Grandma Kata oversaw the farm. Her six kids helped harvest the chicken eggs, clean the coop, hoe and plant the garden, and execute the weekly egg route into the city. I believe Grandma Kata counted me as kid number seven.

It was there, at Grandma Kata's house, where we toiled away at the banner and the hat and the outfit—where we schemed. Those months collapsed onto each other, leading, finally, to this day.

We were six hours early for the concert, not a single butt occupying a single folding chair. We surveyed the rows and rows of empty seats, at the big round stage with temporary backing. It looked like a fair before the fair. We were novices at this, but that wasn't what we thought. "This is how the groupies do it," Aunt Gigi said.

We watched. We walked. We noticed. At first, it seemed like we were all alone, crazy early for a late afternoon concert, nothing to gain but choice seats. Then our eyes adjusted, like how spotting a single ant leads you to discover a whole colony. We noticed people going in, going out—stagehands, they must have been, and equipment managers. The stage door, in particular, was the focal point of the activity at that early hour, and that's where we were camped out.

This was a more intimate time. Security was minimal. Nobody shooed you away unless you were in the way. But I still wasn't the kind of kid to push myself backstage. I was shy, so shy that I'd started going to North Side Hospital where a psychiatrist would prompt me to color pictures that presumably would provide clues into my unease with classmates and other children my age. Social skills would never come naturally to me. One time later, in the fourth grade, Ms. Klimko cornered the whole class to ask, "Why aren't you nice to April?" They saw me as weird. I just didn't fit in. But my special relationship with Frankie had given me confidence, and I had made two playmates on the block. I remember cranking open our jalousie windows, and letting the breeze run across my body, naked except for my white lace panties, and thinking that the world outside was coming to me, and soon I would go to it.

So I was shy. But I was also adorable. All decked out in my Look-At-Me-Frankie! ensemble, I got coos and awwws and clucks. Everybody noticed, everybody admired, cute little me! As an hour passed, then two, the serenity turned to commotion, and all of a sudden, there was Frankie Valli, looking at me.

"Isn't she cute?" he said.

Before I knew it, we were backstage—not long, just a gesture, but *backstage*! At that time, the summer of 1964, everything was crunched together—instead of a Green Room, radio and tech people and everybody else all claimed bits of space. But Frankie had a "private" room, and he let us into that inner sanctuary. Frankie gave me some pumpkin seeds before sending us back to our seats, pumpkin seeds I held tightly in my little hand until Grandma Kata pried them away and put them in a plastic bag.

Without knowing how, I was now a tiny Frankie fan in a

crowd of Frankie fans, the rock concert noise now merging with the amusement park noise to form an absolute din—tinkles and titters, bangs and bellows, gongs and guffaws. Then the brief silence, followed by thunderous applause, and then the Four Seasons and Frankie smoothing the air with their beautiful pop music. By then, I had memorized all of Frankie Valli's songs, listening to my albums on that pink-and-white record player. *Dawn (Go Away) and 11 Other Great Songs* had come out earlier that year, and I'd begged until Mom bought it for me. On that album cover, Frankie and The Seasons, in matching pink shirts, waved as they twisted in their canvas directors' chairs toward the camera. That day at Cedar Point, Frankie did the title track from that album, and he also did the just-released and all-over-the-radio "Rag Doll." I sang and sobbed, sobbed and sang. He went through the rest of the repertoire, a repertoire that I would soon memorize, down to the finale, "Bye, Bye, Baby."

When Frankie broke into the penultimate song, "Let's Hang On," Grandma Kata pushed me toward the stage. Frankie came over, picked me up without missing a beat, held me for a second, and put me down with a gentle hug, at which point I flew back to Grandma Kata.

Before nodding off to sleep on that long drive home, I begged Grandma Kata to take me to another concert. Had Frankie not noticed me in the crowd that night, maybe my fascination would have waned. Maybe I would have discovered the Beatles, or Ricky Nelson, maybe even The Kinks. Maybe my album collection would have grown and grown, until the Four Seasons were just a small part of it. But Frankie *did* notice me.

"You have to wait," Grandma Kata said. "Next summer, we'll go to another. We'll find one, I promise."

*April working in the yard near her playhouse.*

# LOST AND FOUND

On hot summer Sundays after church, when we couldn't stand another sticky minute inside the house, we would go for drives with Grandma Kata. We would take unfamiliar roads in a deliberate attempt to get lost, the game being to find our way back home again. Everything closed down on Sundays in Libertyville, and this served as recreation or entertainment. It started the way it always starts, with Grandma Kata declaring, "Let's get lost!"

It was the summer of 1966. Beautiful, glorious, Ohio summer, a time immortalized in my mind as joyful and serene and exciting. All those summers run together as one glorious event, the event of childhood, and though this was the time between second and third grade, it might have been any of them until those blurred and streaked memories became more shape specific in my teenage years.

It was me, Grandma Kata, Aunt Rosie, and Aunt Ginny, piled into our 1964 Chrysler—no air conditioning, no radio, just us girls. Grandpa Bumpy was so absorbed in the Detroit Tigers radio broadcast he would hardly know we'd gone. Grandma Kata drove. We kicked up dust on a parched August road, Aunt Ginny pointing and shrieking, "Let's go this way!" Tires churned onto gravel and Aunt Rosie ordered, "Turn left."

Church that morning had been exhausting. We believed you had to be saved to go to heaven, and Sundays were work toward that enlightened goal. The end of the world was coming, that much was clear, and we all prepared for the rapture. Church impressed upon me the blight of the world, the worsening crisis of morality and sin, and only in church did I fear for my salvation. We all went and played our roles. Les ushered; Aunt Rosie sang in the choir; I slumped politely in my white lace dress with white bow, staring down at my pink lace anklet socks and black patent leather shoes; and my baby brother, Jeffrey, swaddled in a pale blue sweater and matching blanket, sipped his bottle.

Yes, I now had a baby brother, Jeffrey Lynn, a red, bawling lump of flesh who helped solve some of our family troubles while causing new, wholly unforeseen ones. He was eight years younger than me, which seemed like a large distance even though the gap between Aunt Gigi and I was even greater.

The corn shot way up in the cornfields, over my short little head by a long way, and that corn helped obscure our vision, ahead and behind. Pumpkins dotted the landscape orange. "Turn, turn, turn," I joined in, but Grandma Kata said, "Let's go a little farther."

We Pentecostals were strict and unforgiving; we knew that the Catholics and Jews and everybody else were wrong, we were right, and only through our specific scriptures could we achieve salvation. Everybody else was, literally, damned to hell.

Sunday services were at the Stambaugh Auditorium, where I'd first met Frankie Valli. Being there, week in and week out, reminded me of Frankie, and in the hours between 10 a.m. and 2 p.m., when Mom demanded good behavior while the adults saved their own souls and the souls of everyone they deemed worthwhile, I thought of him. Wearing an expression that others might have interpreted as religious reflection, tucked inside a big velvety chair, I remembered his pool of dark eyes, his mop of black hair, his smile, his voice, his kindness.

That morning at church, before we took off wheeling through cornfields in Grandma Kata's car, a stooped old man, who seemed to me to be about a hundred years old, was invited to the stage so Kathryn Kuhlman could lay hands on him and heal him of his crippling arthritis. We all prayed for him. Kathryn Kuhlman was a well-known healer, and you could bring her just about any problem—multiple sclerosis, ALS, cancer, blindness—and she would lay hands on you, cure you.

Mom—who would have slapped me down, or Jeffrey, if either of us made a peep—sobbed through all of this, though it was hard to say whether she was weeping for the old arthritic man or herself. Lots of people cried during the church service, and for Mom, I think it was a relief to let go of the waterworks without causing embarrassment, criticism, or concern, as was so often the case at home or school or the grocery store—even at work, I imagine. There were a thousand people at these Sunday services—Kathryn Kuhlman was known far and wide—and Mom's snivels were drowned in the general pandemonium.

In the car, we were studying the still roadside stands, and tried to remember signs that read *Fresh Strawberries For Sale* and *Flowers*. We made mental notes of old-looking houses and car makes and yapping dogs. These would be our landmarks, clues that would help us find our way home. "Left, then right!" we ordered.

By that summer, we were out of our little apartment and into our own house a block down the road from Grandma Kata's. The troubles at home, however, hadn't gotten any better; they might've even gotten worse, if that were possible. Les got canned from the Liberty Police Department. He had allegedly exposed himself in front of a woman's window, an accusation he denied. But regardless of the truth, the incident caused a scandal in our cloistered, incestuous community, and now, behind our backs, people gossiped not only about Mom's many affairs but also Les's apparent perversion. He swapped being a cop for being a furniture mover at Harbor's, but in short order he would get his Local 207 Union card and start work in the lucrative steel construction industry, where the overtime seemed endless. But being employed did nothing to help his fits of rage. Instances of him banging cars off the road—his ex-wife's and now Mom's– were legendary, our own *Wonder Years* version of road rage and domestic violence rolled into one.

Even Grandma Kata, once back in the spring, let loose a rebuke—not just of Les, whom everybody in my family strongly disliked, but of Mom. She went on about Mom's bad behavior— she was talking about her many sexual romps—and then scolded me. Even at that age, I tried hard to distinguish myself from Mom. In response to the humiliation of having a different last name than Mrs. Beverly Thomas, I got good grades. When school secretaries, processing another early dismissal, looked down their snooty smart eyeglasses, I "Yes, Ma'am'ed" them. I dressed nice, walked with a perfect posture, and always said my prayers.

I slapped Grandma Kata in the face, instantly sorry and forced to confront, just for a short time, the fact that my stab at "normal" wasn't yet a success.

Our new house at 1241 Townsend Ave. had a Youngstown, Ohio, address, even though we were really in Liberty Township. It was a brick ranch house, three small bedrooms, one bathroom— an ample home, though one that did not compare favorably to those of my classmates. There was a patio out back, and one day a few months after my first backstage encounter with Frankie Valli, I sat under the beautiful blue umbrellas, painting my toes shimmery white, thinking, "We have a house. We have a yard.

Soon, we'll have the rest."

At church that morning, as I watched the arthritic old man get healed, I wondered what other kinds of miracles Kathryn Kuhlman might possibly work. I was thinking about Frankie, or, more specifically, me and Frankie. Just as Grandma Kata had promised, she had found another Frankie Valli concert for us to go to; several, actually. One was at Cleveland's Front Row Theatre—we'd shown up, scouted our advantage, and eventually Grandma Kata had said, "Send the hat back." That old politician's hat, freshened up with new purple FRANKIE glitter, was our all-access pass. Soon, I was backstage again, all wide eyed as Frankie propped me on his lap during a radio interview. Afterward, he cooed, "Are you being a good girl?" And "How is school?" I don't remember what I said, if anything, just the feeling of being on top of the world.

The next one was at the Newcastle Cathedral, where Aunt Ginny and I dressed in identical outfits. We again sent the hat back, and I was invited backstage after the concert. By now, the routine was set: I was the cute little mascot, costume and all. Frankie showed me to the food in a room I understood to be for very important people, and asked, "How did you like the show?" and, "Did you like the new song?" He also said something that stuck with me, then and for a long time. "Always stay beautiful," he said. "You're growing up to be a beauty."

There was another concert coming up at the Sharon High School gymnasium in Pennsylvania, a sports arena-type place where national acts such as the Lettermen had played. Then there would be the Packard Music Hall, Akron Civic Theater, Blossom Music Festival, E.J. Thomas Hall, Heinz Hall, Melon Arena, Pittsburgh Post-Gazette Pavilion, and more.

Between concerts, I worked. Self-improvement was a hot industry then: *The Magic of Thinking Big*, self-hypnosis, unlocking human potential. I was its target audience. I learned and practiced the 4 P's: Plan, Prepare, Pray, and Picture Winning.

It was an inside-outside thing, but my family, my community, and my world best understood the outside. When I pictured *Winning*, I saw a happy Mom, a Mom pleased with all I did for her, with who I was. And now my picture of *Winning* included a close relationship with Frankie. I bought into, truly believed, that good people won. But Bumpy reminded me, "April, there's always someone younger and prettier coming up behind you, so make the best of what you have going."

At seven years old, I'd started taking baton and jazz dance classes at the Nyann School of Dance in Austintown, Ohio. Grandma Kata drove me, a half-hour trek, back and forth, back and forth. Nyann was beautiful, and I listened, practiced and learned from her. She had a big studio, and a dozen or so of us little aspiring performers dutifully played protégé to Nyann's mentor. We learned cool little hip hops, all the basic twirls, even some vaguely dirty dancing. I got so good at baton that Grandma Kata took me to Ravenna to study with Jeanne Flick, one of the best twirling instructors in Ohio. I learned jazz from Tony Romeo and Judy Conti. This was after school, at night, the beginning of my period of grooming. Each time I saw Frankie, I liked to think I was a little better, a little stronger, a little more beautiful.

Some kids collected stamps or marbles, traded baseball cards, grabbed up souvenir plates from every state they'd visited. I collected Frankie, building a shrine to my ever-evolving relationship with the pop star: signed concert programs and music lineups, those pumpkin seeds he'd given me, old ticket stubs, all his records, the April and Frankie dolls and their endless accessories, fan magazine photos and articles. Keep in mind, I was a little girl. My obsession was not of the creepy variety, and I had no sense of where this all would lead, or even what I wanted out of it. I just knew that I had to have the guitar pick, and, oh, I really wanted the press photo. I suppose this was my way of keeping Frankie in my life, having him in my home.

We were hitting pavement now, asphalt being just another

sign of modernization in our humble agricultural community, another way to connect us to the enormous world beyond us. Aunt Ginny giggled, and it was good to have her to myself again. She was a married woman now. Johnny Farcas, a puny, pug-nosed Lebanese man about seven, eight years Aunt Ginny's senior, took my precious aunt away from me, though not for very long. Johnny and Aunt Ginny had met at the First Christian Assembly in Girard, near the newsstand where we'd hunted Frankie concert news. Aunt Ginny, only 20 then, did what girls like her did, girls forbidden from salacious adolescent activities like dancing, playing cards, watching R-rated movies, and sex (God forbid!): she hitched up first chance she got. But Johnny and Aunt Ginny took me everywhere, so much so that everybody thought I was Aunt Ginny's daughter. Still. It was better just the two of us, or the two of us plus Grandma Kata and Aunt Rosie.

"How are we *ever* going to get back?" Grandma Kata teased, one hand on the steering wheel and one propped on the side view mirror, her arm hanging out of the open window.

Johnny and Aunt Ginny had built a little house right across from Grandma Kata's house, and now I was so close that I walked or rode my bike back and forth as my heart desired. My Schwinn bike was still pink and white, but I was moving into a brighter phase. My blush was red, and my new psychedelic bedspread was infused with rose and veronica. In my sight, as I coasted down the big hill, was the maple tree planted the day I was born, just at the end of Grandma Kata's gravel drive. Uncle Bill, Mom's brother and oldest of six, sometimes called me, "Maple Syrup."

We weren't all under the same roof, but it was close, and I whiled away summers pogo sticking, playing dolls, swinging on the aluminum swing set Bumpy had built, dusting the table in my playhouse, going over the hill to catch crayfish, helping with minor chores, being a bigger part of Grandma Kata's household than my own.

Les was gone a lot of the time at my house, but when he was

home, it was understood that we were not to be alone together. This unspoken rule dated all the way back to the beginning of Les, and lasted all the way to the end.

Les could fly off the handle at a moment's notice. The people closest to him knew it and were concerned. At one point, Les's brother and sister, Betty and Bill Thomas, stormed our house for an intervention. They wanted Les to get help, so he could stop losing his temper, stop losing his jobs, stop losing his reputation. They thought his problems related to an ongoing struggle with the trauma of childhood molestation. But Les denied such a thing had ever happened.

It was quite a powwow, with more victims of childhood molestation than I could count:

- Les, who'd been beaten, locked in the cellar and dark closets, and generally abused as a child, had been made to watch his parents have sex.

- Grandma Kata had supposedly been raped by her drunkard surrogate father, who was also her biological uncle. Grandma Kata's biological mother, my Aunt Marie, paid for her care, but when the money ran short, the adoptive parents threatened to put young Grandma Kata on the street. After being molested, Grandma Kata ran away, soon becoming pregnant and administering the first of many coat-hanger abortions.

- Mom had been raped by Bumpy, her stepfather, down on the potato sacks in the basement, and also in the barn. This apparently went on for years.

- Aunt Lerene was also raped by Bumpy, who was also her stepfather. Also for years. Mom and Lerene were the daughters of Frank Burkett.

- Uncle Ronny fought with Bumpy and ran away from home, though nobody knows for sure the reason why. (Uncle Bill, Grandma Kata's first son, had also run away from home; when he got arrested for stealing a car, the judge let him pick between jail and college).

It had been done to all of them, a whole family whose innocence had been violently stolen.

I hardly knew any of this then. All these fuzzy atrocities, and many others, came to me in bits and pieces, but my youthful ignorance, and perhaps a natural naiveté that would last and last, allowed my deep love and trust for my family to continue unabated. What I heard then did not register as condemnation of Bumpy or anybody else; mostly what I got out of it was a looming sense of sadness. The past, for me, in no way impacted my present, and so for me it was a matter of getting through a bad scene to get to a happier one. Maybe I clung to family so tightly because ours was, in reality, so tenuous.

Still, these were good times—or, at least, good enough, after I put out of my mind the image of Mom locked in the bathroom, sobbing and touching up her bruised face; or the memory of waiting at the hospital as Mom got her chipped tooth fixed; or the time Les pounced on Mom for wearing only a house coat in front of our ultra-modern glass sliding doors.

We were zigging and zagging our way into nowhere. There on the horizon, we saw a blue front door on a whitewashed house, white Pricilla curtains tied back, a horse and buggy tethered out back. "There is an Amish house," Grandma Kata said. "We'll remember that."

Grandma Kata's house gave me security. I could go there when things got tense in our new house, like when Mom would rage, "I'm going to divorce you," or when Mom became indignant over Les clocking the mileage on her new navy blue LaSabre, or on the many occasions she would toss his clothes about the house, pack them up, and throw them into the car. There was a running joke around the neighborhood that Les's clothes knew all by themselves how to walk from the closet to the car.

Mom's sadness was matched only by her fatigue, or maybe the

two were intertwined. She left for work at the Hewlett-Packard assembly plant at 4:30 a.m. during the school year, coming home with her white skin cracked from black tape, her whole day spent stooped in front of a conveyor belt as wiring harnesses marched toward her. Grandma Kata came up every morning and slept on the couch until she got me ready for school. But summers, Mom found a way to wiggle out of work. All-day, all-week standing had left her with a bum leg, and she would get a vein in her leg operated on to relieve the pressure. Insurance paid for the procedure and work gave her time off for disability. The first year was easy, even the second, but as Mom reprised the trick a third, fourth, and fifth year, it became a tougher sell. She found co-conspirators in doctors who loved her for her beauty and also, I suspect, for her sexual favors. So she would come home from the operation, plop down on the sofa with her feet up, and be home with us. Those were the times the family felt, to me, whole. She laughed when she didn't cry, and even during those schoolgirl years, I felt a maternal response to seeing her head buried in a washrag, along with a child's naïve hope that I could bring back the happiness. I made Mom glitter cards quoting scripture, scribbled notes about God's love and comfort, and drew pictures of the two of us going away together. I tried, in my own way, to be the adult. When Mom said she hated Mother's Day because motherhood was a thankless job, I hugged her curvy hips and said, "I'm thankful for you."

We prayed on these things in the morning, the lazy summer afternoons, and at bedtime. Mom would say, "In the name of Jesus Christ, come into this child's life right now, fill her with the Holy Spirit. In Jesus' name we pray." Or Grandma Kata would pray, "Put a wall of fire around her so no harm will come to her, lead her, guide her, protect her. Always, today and forever, in Jesus' name we ask, Amen."

When the velvet pouch had made its rounds, we were almost done at Kathryn Kuhlman's. I wasn't saved, exactly; at least not yet, but I'd made a down payment. I eyed the pulpit on the gospel side of the church, and when I blinked could transform Stambaugh back and forth between the different frenzies of rock hall and holy place of worship. Mom's envelope floated into the pouch, fulfilling her obligation to tithe a tenth of her paycheck to the church. The organ swelled. The priestly procession passed.

Then we all shuffled off, free to get lost again.

"Drive toward the sun!" Aunt Rosie offered.

*April and Aunt Ginny leaving a Frankie Valli concert.*

*April at modeling school in Pittsburgh.*

# THE MYSTERIES OF
# MY UNIVERSE

It's hard to pinpoint when I stopped believing in Santa Claus, or how long I let myself be deceived after doubts crept into my maturing mind. But I can still recall, a half-century later, that magical feeling when my eyes blinked open and I realized it was Christmas.

The Youngstown winters were long and harsh, with only little rays of sunshine brightening a speckled path to spring. Our landscape confirmed Grandma Kata's belief that joy was the exception to a mostly subdued life. Beautiful, massive snowfalls started around Thanksgiving and hit us regularly for months and months and months, not a speck of green until May's renewal.

Waiting for the school bus at the end of our crooked gravel street amounted to a Midwestern lesson in 'Toughening Up.' Sometimes Gigi was there waiting for me with dry gloves and we sang songs all the way home. Other times, a red-winged blackbird served as my escort, its red and yellow stripes flashing above; I waited for her and she for me.

I studied hard, and my clearest memory of those winters was the tedious task of writing spelling words over and over until I'd mastered them. *Voyage*: v-o-y-a-g-e. *Graceful*: g-r-a-c-e-f-u--l. *Beautiful*: b-e-a-u-t-i-f-u-l. I went on the occasional sled ride, dutifully practiced twirling and dance lessons, ice skated on the pond behind Grandma Kata's house, and went to church. Mostly, though, it was hard: a lot of time indoors, looking out at a blanket of white purity that soon became corrupted, ever more speckled in nasty crusts of yellows, blacks, and ugly grays.

All that hardness was made tolerable thanks to the pure joy that we'd wait for and then remember: the joy of Christmas!

Christmas was our salvation: the anticipation, the preparation, the excitement, the day itself. I would always get sick with the flu from it all. The Christmas school concert, the church services, and the music of Alvin and the Chipmunks drove me into a full-blown frenzy, leaving me with a red nose like Rudolph and a pasty pale complexion as white as the snow.

It started, of course, very early, way before Thanksgiving even. Aunt Ginny and I sprayed pine cone trees in gold and red; made wreaths; folded and painted cards; Scotch taped hundreds of twinkle lights all over Grandma Kata's house; and arranged plastic candles on the sides of the front door. We'd order gifts with the S&H Green Stamps we'd hoarded over many trips to participating gas stations and grocery stores, and finally pay off the last installments of our special Hills Department Store and Robert Halls layaway items so we could collect in time for the big holiday. We were all over Christmas.

It was Christmas morning, 1968. I had turned 11 earlier in the month, and was halfway through fifth grade. I must have known, or suspected, that Santa Claus was a mythical figure, but it was my way to deny reality long after it had been exposed to the root. I felt the surge of adrenaline, going from sleep to 60 mph in about point four seconds, and then I was there in front of the tree, the red and green and yellow lights splashing the Santa Mouse pajamas I'd gotten as part of our Christmas Eve ritual (pajamas that would soon turn silkier, lacier), my hair in sponge rollers, my mouth agape. Jeffrey Lynn was a toddler, old enough to enjoy but too young to be a co-conspirator in the pre-dawn euphoria. The shiny wraps and bows and silvery tinsel provided an aura of fantasy, and as my eyes adjusted in the faint light—half artificial, half the work of the rising sun peeking through our Townsend Avenue front windows—I spotted the prize among other prizes, the one gift that yelled loud enough to be heard over the din of so many screaming, pleading presents.

*Mystery Date.*

It was a board game I knew about from the annual J.C. Penny's catalogue, and from friends, all of whom agreed it was something we must have, each and every one of us. But nobody had, until *now.* Somewhere behind me was the rustle of Mom shuffling her slippers over our carpet, and Jeffrey squeaking for attention. I blocked all that out and started reading the back of the box.

"The object of the game is to acquire a desirable date, while avoiding the 'dud.' The player must assemble an outfit by acquiring three matching color-coded cards, which then must match the outfit of the date at the 'mystery door.' The date is revealed by spinning the door handle and opening the plastic door on the game board. The five possible dates are the 'formal dance' date, the 'bowling' date, the 'beach' date, the 'skiing' date, and the 'dud.' The date to be avoided is the poorly dressed 'dud.' He is wearing slovenly attire, his hair is tousled, and his face sports a *beard shadow.* If the player's outfit does not match the date behind the door, the door is closed and play continues."

For me, of course, the Dream Date was Frankie. I was ready to play. Mom, though, insisted I put aside the game—there would be time for playing and prancing and exploring later. Now, we had to open all the gifts, and then move through our day.

My Christmases, during those grade school years, were divided into three parts: mornings on Townsend Avenue; Christmas afternoon in Niles, Ohio, with Dad and that side of the family; and evenings at Grandma Kata's house.

It was 35 minutes in the car from Liberty to Niles, and Dad said precious little on the drive. His mousy frame barely filled the driver's seat, his manicured hands caressed the wheel, his nervous eyes surveyed the road. Mom always said there were two kinds of Italian men: Mama's Boys and Arrogant Runarounds. Dad was a Mama's Boy. Soon, I was standing on Anne Street in my winter coat, muff, and white fur hat, clutching my little apple-red pocket book. Then I was strolling up the walk on Mason Street following Dad to pay my respects to relatives I didn't much know or understand. Every house was filled with Italian immigrants that congregated in Niles because of the steel mills: here for jobs—*good* jobs—here for what they hoped and believed was a better life. Most seemed somehow related to me and Dad. The Prezziosos, the Vellecos, Aunt Carmel, my godfather Uncle Paul. I was playing with first and second and third cousins, or in the orbit thereof.

Dad, after the divorce, took occupancy in his mom's (Grandma Gatta's) house, and during our once-every-other-week visits we would sit in her basement while he played sax or clarinet numbers, as he had in the Army band. Grandpa Gatta played accordion. Grandpa and Grandma Gatta migrated from Bologna, and neither spoke English; she called me "Ah Pril." Yet despite the language barrier, both my grandparents on Dad's side made it crystal clear that they hated Mom. Sometimes Dad's sisters, Aunt Rose, who lived across the street, or Aunt Netta, who lived in Alliance, would translate. They'd listen to the rat-a-tat melodies, the rising and falling accents, watch all the hand gestures, then turn to me and repeat, "Your mother took you away from us. Your mother is a bad person." Or, "We had a big wedding for your mother. She was never happy."

Dad was 12 years older than my mom, 32 the year I was born. He was a tiny man, short, well dressed, with beautiful, black hair and coal-black eyes. He came across as elegant. Elegant and meek. Dad would have sooner cut off his own arm than speak up. Though I was little, I recall there being some chairs thrown and broken—the only violent episode of their entire marriage—when she wanted me to be baptized Protestant. I was baptized Catholic.

I suppose their marriage was doomed from the start. Dad took all their wedding money and bought a clothing store that failed miserably, not so much draining as flushing their meager savings, and in short time, a mysterious fire made ashes out of the dreams, ashes that at least brought back something from the insurance. Years later, Mom confided that she had told Dad she wanted a divorce because he did not fulfill her sexually, a proclamation I can only imagine Dad accepted without dispute. Dad still worked in a clothing store called Strouss that would later turn into Kaufmann's, then Macy's.

When Mom had broken the news to me about the divorce, she'd spun it this way: "You'll get double gifts. All this is double now."

Four hours, that was our allotted time together at Christmas, father and daughter; and I think, for both of us, that was plenty.

After making the rounds to Anne and Mason Streets, and other stops in between, we ended up across the street from Grandma Gatta's. Aunt Rose had tons of kids, how many, I could only guess. Whenever I went there, all the music and human voices and clanking dishware rattled my teeth, especially when I went there at Christmas. There was lots of food, like leftover fish and macaroni, and I more tolerated than enjoyed this middle part of the festivities. I wanted my Daddy, and he foisted me off on my cousins.

I was always relieved to go back home, and on that 35-minute return trip, my fatigue would again turn to excitement as I thought about Grandma Kata's evening celebration. As I looked over at Dad, his face concentrated on the road, I studied his hair, his features, his hands. That first time in concert, I immediately recognized that Frankie looked like Dad, but now I wondered if it wasn't Dad who looked like Frankie.

Throwing off my coat and sliding out of my itchy leotards, kicking my black patent leather shoes into the corner, I could smell the big turkey roasting, almost taste the stuffing. I hugged Grandma Kata and kissed Mom. My two cousins, Kathy and Terie, were waiting for me, and we put black olives on our fingertips and danced around the kitchen. Dinner always came first, an absurd number of people crowded around a long table, adjacent tables scooched together, chairs wedged in, until it became a sort of tent city with way more occupants than land. As delicious and raucous and fun as that meal was, I hurried through, hoping to set a frenetic pace so that we could get to the main event. At the kids' table, we discussed what we got that morning. Mashed potatoes floated like clouds on our plates, and moms orbited with bowls and ladles and pitchers. *Who wants gravy? White meat?* Pumpkin pies, my favorite food of all, cooled on the counter top, waiting until after gifts were opened. Soon, we furiously cleared the table, stacked dishes in the sink, and ran to the TV room.

The tree glowed, a sort of majestic quality to which I think we all aspired. There were too many presents to describe. Grandma Kata had six kids, and now many of them had spouses, children of their own; at one point, I had three girl cousins born within a year. Bumpy handed out the presents, and we unwrapped them one at a time, nobody allowed to start on another until the last one was done, displayed, *oohed* and *aaahed* over, thanks given to the appropriate relatives.

We took Polaroid shots of the most special presents, and

waited for the image to develop, click, and stutter its way to reality. All this took forever, but it seemed to pass in a snap. I got Frankie Valli albums; more Barbie stuff; Go Go boots to wear to my next Frankie concert; a toy of the cartoon mouse Topo Gigio, who somehow also reminded me of Frankie. Aunt Ginny told me she was going to take me to a Frankie concert next summer— that was my gift. The other kids and the women made out like bandits, as well, while the men, all of them, got work clothes and work gloves, like every Christmas. With my new haul piled up in front and behind, off to the sides, so many gifts that I stood as though in a cocoon of Christmas gifts, I still thought of *Mystery Date*, which I'd secretly snuck into our car so we could hopefully play later.

Toward the end, when the pretty square and cylindrical and rectangular wrapped gifts morphed into a huge pile of crumpled paper, Bumpy ceremoniously gave Grandma Kata her gift: a wedding ring, at last!

Bumpy, the head of the family, had never naturalized. He came to Grandma Kata in the literal dark of night, under the assumed name of "John Thomas," on the run from the law for his work in Warren, Ohio as a petty thief, whore handler, and who knew what else. It was years until anybody, least of all Grandma Kata, knew that he was a Polish immigrant, John Kata. He'd come, that first time, to this beautiful spot in the woods, a perfect hiding place, his suits and shoes and monogrammed shirts and fake birth certificate all labeled "John Thomas."

This was a time of vulnerability and stress, when Grandma Kata, a single mother of three, had already divorced once and sent her second true love off to World War II. Bumpy, with charisma and a stable, well-paying steel mill job, lucked into perfect timing to win Grandma Kata, as well as his permanent hideout in the beautiful wooded back lot. When the police eventually came they were looking for John Kata, not John Thomas. The police kept getting redirected to his mom's house across town.

But in those childhood years, I knew little if any of this backstory. Bumpy spent most of his home time huddled around the basement furnace, where he would sometimes surreptitiously burn papers and artifacts no doubt related to his shady past. This was a boon time for immigrants, some of whom tended to blow their disposable steel mill pay on liquor, prostitutes, gambling, and other such stuff considered in some circles to represent the good life. Bumpy had profited off providing that good life, but not anymore. Now, he worked, played the stock market, and slid into that past only occasionally, maybe during his regular Friday night poker games in Bomb Town, USA, or when he pilfered goods from the local department store, Stambaugh-Thompson.

Grandma Kata, too, was changed, in large part due to the fact that she'd found God and rejected her youthful self, the stunning woman who could and would seduce just about any man. Grandma Kata had been given away at birth. Her mom, my great grandma, was Teacher of the Year in Ohio, and unwed pregnant women could not then be teachers at all, much less Teachers of the Year. Grandma Kata, her head misshapen because Great Grandma had strapped her unborn baby in a dangerously tight corset, went to live with an aunt already burdened with children of her own and with a drunkard husband. Grandma Kata's head had to be massaged back into shape. She was an unwanted baby who would be abused and humiliated. She ran away from home; gave birth to Bill, a baby she could not afford to keep; found him a foster home in Cleveland run by a couple willing to take care of Bill until Grandma Kata could reclaim him. In the meantime, she had to pay all the baby's bills. Grandma Kata took on jobs as a house cleaner, and walked—*nearly 70 miles one way*—to the foster home each weekend.

Eventually, she got Bill back; married Frank Burkett, a dancer; produced my mom (Beverly), Ronnie, and Lerene; divorced Frank Burkett, who would die in New York City from alcoholism at age 42; and fell in love with Paul Galetti, who was shipped off to fight in the Second World War. Somewhere in there were a handful of coat-hanger abortions. Somewhere in there also was a scene in which Frank Burkett returned home, girlfriend on his arm, to name Lerene, who found out later he was not truly her biological father. Then came Bumpy, who in Grandma Kata saw not a beaten but a wild woman—a woman who drank men under the table, screwed at her leisure, sang and danced and cursed.

Then came Ginny. Then Rosie, born so premature that the doctor advised depriving her food so she'd be dead by morning. Aunt Rosie survived, but was handed over to Bumpy's mom. Grandma Kata nearly collapsed with depression, Aunt Ginny cried for a year, and Aunt Rosie grew up fragile and afraid.

It got to where a still-young Grandma Kata stood poised to throw herself off a train—enough, apparently, was enough. But then she heard a voice. It was a voice decrying her fate, her reason to live. God, and God alone, was the only potential salvation. Her world turned white and clean, like the Priscilla drapes in the kitchen and the starched sheets on our beds, the farmhouse transformed into sacred ground. All these years later, Grandma Kata had found peace, while Bumpy waxed nostalgic for the vivacious woman who was once his rowdy, robust playmate.

I didn't know about any of that, and I didn't know or understand about Bumpy's molestation of Mom and Lerene.

All these decades later, I don't know how to feel about Bumpy; the way I felt about the person I knew on that Christmas night, or the person I learned about later. Mom always loved him, so much so that when he died she would go, for a long time, to lay on top of his grave. Grandma Kata, too, was so devoted that, at his funeral, despite the appearance of Dapple Blondie, Bumpy's mistress, she just about crumbled.

On this night, the night Grandma Kata got her wedding ring, it looked and felt to my young eyes and heart like Norman Rockwell bliss. I knew Bumpy as quiet and kind, Grandma Kata as strong and determined. The time was coming, two decades hence, when Bumpy and Cousin Kathy would be dead, when so too would be the steel mills. When my high school friends would be locked up one after another, when I would unwittingly follow in the family footsteps, and give up my sweet teenage years to marry. But not yet, not now.

In the other big addition, which we called the piano room, we sang, "Hark the Herald Angels Sing!," "We Wish You A Merry Christmas," and all the standard tunes. "The Twelve Days of Christmas" was a whole family performance, each of us moving our hands and swaying our bodies to mime the five golden rings, the calling birds, all the way down to the partridge in a pear tree.

We were all gathered around the piano that had been given to Aunt Rosie after she quit speaking. She had been playing army with some neighbor boys, out back of Grandma Kata's, when one of the boys was shot to death. Bumpy followed screams of horror into the field and found this seven-year-old boy with a shotgun hole in the middle of his chest. He threw a blanket on him and ran with him up the hill to the boy's house; finding nobody home, he laid the boy on the porch and ran next door. That's how the parents found their son when they pulled up minutes later. After I heard that story, wandering the woods, I tried to determine the exact spot where that little boy had died, hoping not to step on such sad ground. I'm still affected by it. Just kids playing in a field, like any other fall weekend in the country— how could it have turned out so? Aunt Rosie saw a psychiatrist for a long time after that. The piano was therapy, and it worked. Aunt Rosie, timid and unsure, sang Christmas carols like a pretty angel, and performed at churches and old folk homes.

We were all exhausted, almost ready to go home, but I got my way and we broke out *Mystery Date*. My red velvet dress was as itchy as I was to get to this game. It was me, Aunt Ginny, Terie, and Kathy. This was a game, as I saw it, where you got to try dating the man you would eventually date when you grew up, in my case, Frankie Valli. We were four girls, arranging and rearranging the 48 outfits, opening and closing the mystery date door.

I always liked boys, but I was still a few years away from actual, in-the-flesh romance, even of the puppy love variety. My fantasy about Frankie was as real as it got for me, and now, as we played *Mystery Date*, it was he who came as my suitor, he who dressed to impress me, he who took me bowling, he who, eventually, would marry me.

We played until Mom and Les insisted we go, and I cried a bit, knowing Christmas had all but officially ended. Mom told me, "You never give up on love." She said, "Love will never fail you." I believed her, ignoring, as children do, the contrast between Mom's words and the reality that lay bare before me.

On the short ride back to our apartment, just days after the Winter Solstice that signaled the darkest day of the year, I started to nod off. I heard a *thwap!* Startled, I craned my neck over the back seats for a glimpse at headlights trained on a near-barren road. "What was that?" I squealed.

"I killed one of Santa's elves," Les said, chuckling.

*April and Frankie at
Stambaugh Auditorium.*

*April and cousins celebrate
Christmas at Grandma Kata's.*

# GETTING INTO THE GAME

*L is for the way you look at me*
*O is for the only one I see.*
*V is very very extraordinary*
*E is even more than anyone that you adore.*

Mark Sabela was a black-haired Italian boy who sang bass in a gospel group called The Acts, as in *Act I: Jesus Taken Up To Heaven, Act II: The Holy Spirit Comes at Pentecost,* and so forth. His brother, Tommy, six years older, fronted the band as they traveled about the area, singing, passing out tracts, and preaching salvation. I knew Mark from our youth group at First Assembly of God in Youngstown. We went to different schools, so we only saw each other in church, or when I went to see The Acts. I went to church a lot that year.

It was the summer between seventh and eighth grade. I was 13, coming into bloom. I still acted out fantasies with my Frankie and April dolls, popped wheelies on my pink Schwinn, played *Life* with neighbor friends Dawna and Mary. But I could feel the slight tugs of adulthood.

Thirteen. Mom had taken me to Strouss to buy my first bra, a size 6X for children, and after that I was forbidden to wear t-shirts. I got my first period at school, and when I got home, toilet paper stuffed into my panties, Mom marched me down to Gray's Drugstore in Liberty Plaza for tampons. Thirteen. We never, *ever* discussed love or sex or my body, but I could feel things changing. Thirteen. I was just a year younger than Grandma Kata was when she had her first pregnancy. Just four years younger than Aunt Lerene when she had her shotgun wedding. Just five years younger than Mom when she married and, in short order, gave birth to me. Just seven years younger than Aunt Ginny when she had grabbed marriage as a way to get out of the house. Thirteen. In two years, my best friend Dawna would get pregnant.

Biological, genetic, and social imperatives were at work.

I placed in the top five in my first beauty pageant, and though the whole spectacle made me uncomfortable, at least part of me swelled from the attention. I'd worn a beautiful green dress with matching protégé shoes, my hair half back like a princess. I smiled a big smile and made it a point to hold a warm gaze just a beat as I looked directly into each judge's eyes. This was in the center of the concourse, near the food court, in the mall in which my dad sold men's suits. The whole family was there, cheering me on, willing the judges to choose me to be Miss Eastwood Mall over the other three-dozen or so aspiring beauty queens.

What pleased me most was seeing Dad watch me from a distance. Everyone in the mall knew Dad from his job; though such things were never said aloud, I could tell he was proud. I was judged on poise, appearance and personality. I walked for the judges, and answered questions in the manner of a good, caring Christian girl, which I was, and for my efforts I received a small trophy and a gift certificate to be used at my discretion anywhere in the Eastwood Mall.

There had been other flirtations, innocent and never acted upon. In fact, I never thought of myself as flirtatious, it was just the way I was, and maybe for that reason, or maybe because my perky young breasts and slim hips had started to fill out my wardrobe, that a certain David Trebilcock had aspired to win my affections.

That my first sort of romance was with a boy named "Trebilcock" did not strike me then as auspicious or ironic, though my lifetime with men has taught me that they all should be named this way.

David Trebilcock was a "Midwestern Boy" out of central casting: blonde hair, hazel eyes, short and husky, devoted churchgoer, good family stock. Pleasant Valley Church was where we met, and between there and school, we became friends, good friends. I considered David's rash, which broke out horribly all over his body, a flaw, but little did I know that all men were flawed, honestly and truly, and that all *my* men were flawed by the arbitrary fact that they were not Frankie Valli. Later, as I re-imagined my life from a distance and thought about all those paths not taken, David would become the first in a chain of what-ifs. What if I had married David, had a few chubby cherubs, and lived the life of a deacon's wife, playing tennis with my well-bred in-laws, taking jaunts to the family's Florida home, welcoming my hubby with milk and cookies when he returned from work?

While David pursued in the mild way of a nice 13-year-old God-fearer, I veered in the direction of Peter Riberi, wild and bad, a regular puller of pranks, like tossing my beautiful sunbonnet way high up in a tree. While David made kind overtures, Peter called me "Gatta Fatta of the Apes," and made a show of picking me last when kickball teams were chosen. I made it known, through deed if not word, that I preferred the cruel boy to the kind boy, a pattern that, once established, proved hard to break.

Peter was lanky, a maniacal nail biter, with brilliant brown eyes that sparkled when he spoke, full of every kind of mischief possible.

I was sitting in a pew with my other girl church friends when Peter shuffled into church. He excused himself—"excuse me, excuse me, excuse me"—as he deliberately made his way toward—*me*. He sat right next to me. He took my hand. He held it. This was the first time I ever felt my heart race. When it was time to sing, he took the hymnal book out of the holder and shared it with me. We sang together, as one, the rest of the church also joining with our voices but not breaking our spell of intimacy. This was a moment of true connection, the first time my heart raced and hands sweated, and I basked in the moment as the music blended magically with the man, a union that would forever be my weakness, though the songs and faces changed, *click click*, like a beautifully scored tribute.

After that, there were many phone conversations, a few stolen kisses, and once, on a cold, wintry voyage to Toledo, Ohio, an awkward backseat make out session. Mom allowed me to go to all the church activities, and that became our chance to be a couple. In the backseat of his brother's car, on the way to see a gospel group called The Imperials, Peter and I floundered about, trying to figure out, together, how this was done.

Peter ultimately meant little to my life, except that my innocent love affair with him made complete my transition from girl to young woman. Sex did not yet enter my head—I was too pious and naïve for any of that. I watched *The Monkees* and *The Partridge Family* on TV, and accelerated my schedule of walking, talking, speech-making, and dancing classes. My mother wanted me to be a beauty queen, and I wanted what Mom wanted. It was not until college that I would even dare utter a swear word, afraid to violate Mom's principles.

There was just one Frankie concert that year, 1971. His career had hit a lull. He had some concerts in England but not many in the U.S. With a reduced tour schedule, my chances to see him were few and far between. The Four Seasons had come out with a new album, *Half & Half*, the previous year. I dutifully bought it, but none of the songs became hits, and soon I went back to playing his earlier albums. But Frankie was coming to Buffalo's Kleinhans Music Hall in March, and I *had* to be there.

Mom went to the Italian lady's house on Fifth Avenue in Youngstown to have her tailor for me a double-breasted velvet jacket, a little skirt, and a ruffled blouse. She was the same lady who had made an earlier version of the velvet jacket, as well as my pageant gown. We went to Baker's Shoes to complete the ensemble.

I went to Buffalo with Aunt Ginny and my girlfriends, bragging the whole way how I knew Frankie, overwhelmed with the fear that he might not recognize me. But I had The Hat, and I had the velvet jacket that matched the velvet jacket Frankie had worn at various concerts and also on the *Looking Back* album cover, in which he sported a goatee and jeans, posed on railroad tracks. I had grace, I had poise, I had all the manners a young girl needed to become a proper young woman.

The hat worked, like it always worked, and good thing. Frankie was a star, an important person, and my relationship with him somehow made me special, made me important. Had I not been acknowledged or welcomed, the opposite would have been true, and at that fragile moment in my existence, I don't know how I would have handled such a truth.

We went backstage and snapped pictures with Frankie, Tommy DeVito, all the Four Seasons. Frankie now had a mustache, and a swirl of gray hair fringing his mop of brown hair. Frankie was 32, almost 33 years old, but I didn't think of it that way. He was a man, not a boy, and that was all the distinction I drew. I was aglow, my friends were impressed, there was joy and music and something like grown-up camaraderie on the ride home, as we giggled our reviews of the whole experience.

The priceless hat, the one and only Frankie hat, went back in the closet in my bedroom, along with the banner and velvet suit. I realized, kneeling down to pray that evening, that I'd gone out on a limb with my friends, and it struck me how awful and humiliating things might have turned out. But they hadn't. *Dear Heavenly Father, I pray for my mom, give me peace, help me with lessons. Dear Heavenly Father, I pray for Frankie and me, if it's meant to be, lead us and guide us and let us learn what love is. If it's your will, let us be together.*

There would be, in the near future, other pageants—Miss Youngstown, Miss Junior Miss, Miss Teen Ohio, Miss Ohio Teen—and other titles—Miss Ohio and sixth runner-up Miss USA. There would be beautiful white shelves in my bedroom, adorned with gold trophies, brown wooden statues, plaques, and ribbons. I suppose all of this, unconsciously, was a continuation of my goal to be pretty, to be accomplished, to be the kind of girl somebody like Frankie Valli would want to make his wife.

I had no idea when I would see Frankie again, and for now I was okay with that. He was not gone, nor was he forgotten, but my priorities had shifted, at least a little. Besides, it felt, with that last concert, that we'd crossed some sort of threshold. This thing with Frankie had always seemed, always was, a force of will, a product of my earnestness and persistence, that without my heroic efforts the relationship would die a quick death. Now, though, I felt some reciprocity, the tiniest hint that Frankie got as well as gave, though what it was he got was unclear to me.

*April and Frankie 1971*

*Barbara Dunning, Grandma Kata and April*
*going to a Frankie Valli concert.*

# ON MY OWN

"Here's the money, just go," Mom said.

Frankie was coming to Stambaugh and though it had been ten years—a full decade—since I'd first seen him, and more than two years since I'd last seen him, there was no doubt in my mind: I was going. Mom was distracted, which might have been a kind way to say, "Whacked out," and Grandma Kata's All-Things-Frankie spirit had fizzled after the last concert. That one was in Newcastle, Pennsylvania, where I'd worn high heels for the first time, and a fitted floral dress that showed my newly blossomed curves. Frankie was very nice, and said, "Look at you! You're growing up! You look great!" He asked me about school, my grades, how I liked the show—he *always* asked how I liked the show. But he was especially—overly?—attentive to Aunt Ginny, a young married beauty. Later, when we were in the audience, I watched Grandma Kata watch Frankie watch a young man posed up in the bleachers. She was circumspect afterward, probably because I was just 14 at the time, but her attitude toward Frankie definitely cooled.

I lay stomach down on my bed, looking through a large window at people coming and going. I'd taken over the master bedroom in the Townsend house, partly because my wardrobe and beauty queen accouterments had grown out of control, partly because I was a country girl, always half naked, and Mom had become increasingly aware of Les watching me as I came in and out of my room. The bathroom was directly across from my room so I could go in and out a thousand times without notice. The big bedroom offered more privacy, more protection.

I was now in an orange-and-black, tiger-stripe phase. I'd taken down all my mice, including Topo Gigio; I'd taken down the white canopy; I'd taken down lacy this and girlish that. I now had a tangerine comforter, tiger orange sheets and pillowcases, sandstone carpeting—all from J.C. Penney. A black and white zebra-striped rug sprawled across the floor. Even the car that Mom and Les got me for my 16th birthday was orange, or, to be more precise, gold. It was this beat-up Chevy, an early-60s model with scrapes and dings and rust. But it was all mine, and I would take that car over bumps and around bends with W.H.O.T. blaring on the radio. The world, I supposed, watched in admiration. No air conditioning, windows that had to be cranked, a scratchy radio. But it was better than the school bus.

Despite this careful color-coordinated décor, my room often looked like a hurricane had blasted through the pages of *Teen*. I'd started to pick up after it, but lost heart. Clothes were everywhere—on the floor, draped over my chair, dangling from the lights framing my makeup mirror, in the closet, folded in stacks near the wall. Paperboy hats, big floppy beach hats, and sun visors hung on my bedposts. Jewelry boxes were scattered throughout the room. My majorette boots with big yarn pom-poms sat near the door, and my letterman's jacket hung on a hook stuck to the closet door.

This is because my clothes competed for closet space with trophies from every pageant in Ohio, from county fairs to regional and national pageants. These pageant companies took all comers, grabbed up high registration fees and lucrative sponsorships, essentially using us budding beauty queens for profit. But at the time, I had not crunched these numbers, and I, with Mom's insistent encouragement, was a carnival go-er, plunking down my dollar to throw balls nearly too big for the basket, hoping to win a prize worth less than the entry fee.

I lifted the large handle from its ornate gold-trimmed pedestal, circled Aunt Ginny's gold numbers on my rotary Princess Phone. I tapped my bare toes on the floor, stroked the fur of my miniature Shih Tzu dog, Lovie, who I had gotten as another bribe, or therapy maybe, after I'd had an emotional breakdown. The psychiatrist said it was due to stress—basically, the cause had been determined to be the pageant circuit. The cure: my own little dog. I'd gone with Mom to Cleveland, where we picked up the adorable animal from a gay couple who'd wanted to find it a good home. I loved it instantly. The previous owners had called the dog Love Bug, and we sort of kept the name, though mostly we used Lovie. We'd had two dogs since Ricky Lynn's tragic death, but Fatty and Bryan were Jeffrey's Golden Labs. Lovie was mine, a little creature I vowed to protect. I would not let what happened to Ricky Lynn happen to Love Bug. I guarded Lovie vigilantly, so vigilantly that some decade and a half later, a veterinarian had to scold me into letting the poor, suffering dog die.

I put the receiver to my ear and listened for Aunt Ginny's voice on the other end.

Then I launched into it: "Gigi? Guess what?" I asked. "I'm getting Frankie tickets! He's at Stambaugh. Come with?"

"No thanks," Aunt Ginny said. "I've got something going that night."

What Aunt Ginny had going was Uncle Chuck—or the future Uncle Chuck, I should say. She had divorced Uncle Johnny, married Uncle Bill Crain, and was now caring for a little toddler, my cousin Heather. They had built a large home together with a built-in pool, pool house, the works. But more and more, it was Uncle Bill at work while Aunt Ginny sneaked around, throwing off the guilt and self-loathing long enough to get her fix. Heather stayed much of the time with Grandma Kata, injecting some joy into the old farm that had dwindled down to a couple of mouser cats and Oscar the saggy little Shepherd half-breed. It was just a matter of time before Uncle Bill heard the news, if he hadn't already.

I was old enough now that I understood the significance and impact of all my family's tangled relationships, though I was too self-absorbed to think of it as much more than drama. It was the summer between my sophomore and junior years, and in both my first two years of high school I'd been named Best Dressed in the yearbook. I wore big, cheap chic sunglasses; hip pocket wallets; sometimes, in defiance of (or maybe revenge toward) my mother, grey Playboy Bunny shirts with a matching baseball cap. I now wore my hair bobbed; I'd dyed blond highlights into my dark hair; I shaved my legs *every* night; my boobs had swelled to a C, which I stuffed into a B cup. I had become a believer in the power of shoes, and lipstick. There was also a pair of white go-go boots and a white fur coat that made their appearances in the winter. It was 1974, and I was conflicted between the outrageous fashion of the times and the prim fashion of my church upbringing. Outrageous was winning out.

But this wild April stayed on the surface, obscuring an earnest, ambitious, God-fearing Inner April, an April overwhelmed with the work of making herself good and noble and successful, and, perhaps, famous, or at least famous on some provincial, Liberty, Ohio scale.

Mom drove me each Saturday to the John Robert Powers Finishing School, where I was enrolled in the charm section. The drive was two hours each way, to downtown Pittsburgh and back. There we learned to walk, talk, use silverware, make introductions. We learned how to turn a doorknob without turning our backs on our audience. We learned the ins-and-outs of social introductions, we read books on grace, and we studied how to color coordinate with our skin tones. Oranges and other warm colors suited me, none of the cool colors, which perhaps explained, in part, my new orange phase.

I was on Joseph Horn's Teen Board, and would go to Boardman, Ohio, to model in all the fashion shows. As a Candy Striper at North Side Hospital, where I was born, I rolled a cart to the various sick rooms to sell candy, breath mints, toothpaste, stuffed animals, and magazines. I was Head Majorette and Featured Twirler for the Leopards, the Liberty High School's marching band. I learned about etiquette and fashion at the Barbizon School of Modeling in downtown Youngstown. I raised money for lots of causes, dialing businesses for sickle cell anemia, carrying the white box for the Red Cross, going door to door for the American Cancer Society. At Christmas, I was always a Santa's Helper. Aunt Rosie and I would also go sing at old folks' homes, lugging our tiny Yamaha box with portable microphones so we could do justice to numbers like "He Lives," "The Old Rugged Cross," and "Because He Lives."

I still practiced walking with books on my head, almost habitually now, since I'd been doing it virtually since I was a toddler—pacing my bedroom, or the path between the bathroom and my bed, on trips down to the breakfast table. Mom still hammered home messages about etiquette, vigilant messages about my posture, my smile, *grace*.

But maybe because of all this self-improvement, all these good deeds, all this reaching for the stars, all this… busyness, I found myself with no real girlfriends. Dawna was soon to be a mom, and I'd edited her out of my life, appalled or shocked or afraid or just plain too immature to confront her new reality. Mary had dropped more or less out of sight. There were plenty of other girls from school, classes, and marching band, with whom I got along just fine. But we never got close. As I scanned my room now, laying there listening to Aunt Ginny rattle on about all the things she would be doing that were not going with me to see Frankie Valli, I noticed, for the first time, that my walls and desks were completely devoid of friends' pictures. No hugging, smiling, silly shots; no reminders of cherished besties; no proof of a sorority to which I belonged. Even my cousins Kathy and Terie, born in the same year, kept me at a distance.

"Come on, Gigi—it's just one night!!!!"

"You go," she said, firmly.

Not that I wasn't popular, in my own way. I'd started making out with boys, holding hands at church, feeling up and getting felt up over our clothes. Boys had started driving by the house; they stole shoes from my locker; took my bras at camp and strung them up.

I hung up the Princess Phone, rolled over onto my back, then popped out of bed. I walked to the closet, reached high onto the top shelf. In the clutter of my fashion emporium, that silly hat—my admission ticket, my entry into Frankie's world—still sat. So many times, I'd shown up with that hat. All I had to say was, "Send the hat back," and soon I was told, "Frankie said he'll see you after the show." Or, "He can come back in an hour." The hat distinguished me from thousands of tiny Frankie fans. Somebody from Frankie's crew would see it, yell, "The girl with the hat is here." The hat was everything.

But that last time, I hadn't brought the hat. That time, I was *The Girl from Youngstown*. With or without the hat, I was recognizable. I heard the crew say, "The girl from Youngstown is here." It had seemed like a graduation, of sorts, but from what to what I could not say.

I thought about calling Dawna, but truthfully, from the moment I'd heard she was pregnant, she'd ceased to exist for me, or at least to exist in any real, human way. It was as though her pregnancy, to me, was death, the death of our friendship, the death of our childhood, the death of the bubble under which we'd been allowed to incubate. What would I say to Dawna, anyway? She'd disappeared from school, and at this point, I didn't even know if she was still pregnant or had delivered the baby. I didn't know if she was home—fatigued from long nights, nursing her precious little one, trying to figure out how her life, and that of another, would proceed—or if she had moved away. I didn't even know whether she kept the baby. Yet, I thought about Dawna now, and some still-youthful part of me almost dialed the phone to ask the stupid question, "Want to go see Frankie with me?"

In all my striving for goodness, it had never once occurred to me that I, Dawna's once-best friend, should try considering what I could do for *her*, how I could ease *her* pain, and not the other way around.

I could ask a boy, but to do so would be interpreted as a date, and part of me knew, way before I knew anything else, that I could not, would not, bring a boyfriend to see My Frankie.

Who then?

I popped into the bathroom, put on my bathing suit, grabbed a towel, assembled a bag, and started out of the house. As I descended the steps I heard Mom sing, "Here she comes… Miss A-mer-i-ca!!!!" an old routine that had become somewhat of a family tradition, Mom still clinging to the truth of such sentiments. I suppose I believed as well, though I was no longer flattered in the way I'd been as a little girl. I waved and sashayed out the glass sliding doors, across the porch, down to the pool.

I emptied out my goodies bag on the glass table: cuticle cream, cuticle stick, emery boards, buffer, scissors, base coat, color, top coat. I munched a pretzel rod and sipped diet Tab. I turned on my transistor radio, which almost, but not quite, drowned out the chlorine filter's trickle and the pool heater's hum.

I'd already removed the old cantaloupe coat and soaked my toes in the tub, each digit growing tender and soft and pliant.

I'd pumice stoned the dead skin. Now I weaved toilet paper in between my toes. I blinked to water my new contacts, and studied each toe as I applied a new coat of yam orange. Little brush strokes to cover the surface of each nail. The pool water rippled gently; my breathing slowed. This was my place of serenity. Jeffrey Lynn's banging, Mom's crying, Les's shouting—it was better for that to be in there, and me to be out here. Today, though, the sun beat down on my head, my breasts, my thighs. My toes warmed as I waited for the first coat of yam to take. A trickle of sweat rolled off my forehead, and my ear itched. The world seemed incredibly large and I incredibly small.

The perfect pedicure requires patience. I waited, listening to HOT 101 FM play scratchy songs that were not Frankie Valli songs, one after another. As I waited, I thought about my dilemma, for it was now that. Seeing Frankie had always been a family affair, but Aunt Ginny was out, Grandma Kata was out, Mom was out. I'd ruled out girlfriends. Ruled out boyfriends.

And yet, it never occurred to me not to go. That left me. Alone.

The Spinners' "One of a Kind (Love Affair)" played, and then Donny Osmond's "Puppy Love". I sang along, not really internalizing the lyrics, or even aware that every note coming out of my transistor addressed some notion of love. Unrequited love. Budding love. Love lost. Sex. The Staple Singers' "I'll Take You There" kicked into high gear, and at that time, in that place, I had no idea about the subtext.

I'd discovered, with boys and with myself, the heat and moisture that tingled below, but here, at the pool, with my cross dangling from my neck, almost reaching my toes as I tried to blow them dry, I did not connect one thing to another.

It had been nearly two years since I'd first pleasured myself. It had been an accidental discovery, lying on my bed. Like most teenagers, I vacillated between the desire for more and a guilt-driven need to stop. I could make myself come almost instantaneously, just a few gentle strokes, a tiny teasing diddle. The release always felt monumental, but then, immediately, I turned orange with anxiety, like a petty thief suddenly realizing, "What have I done? What if somebody finds out?"

I thought about all kinds of things when I satisfied myself, the whole operation deep under the covers so that even I could not see the science involved. But I never thought about Frankie. Never. He had remained a childhood fantasy, somebody to love, somebody to adore, somebody, yes, to marry. But that? No. It never entered my mind.

Finally, as the second coat of yam dried and my toes attained a stylized, manufactured perfection, the DJ announced over the radio, "And now, for all you ladies from the sixties 'til today," and started to play Frankie's "Who Loves You." It was a sign.

I was going to see Frankie at Stambaugh. Just me.

*Canfield Fair Parade.*     *Miss Ohio Teen.*

# SLEEPING WITH FRANKIE

The mirror showed me a hot young woman, dressed in a gauzy creme linen pant suit, bell sleeves, a v-neck top showing a hint of cleavage obscured by layers of gold chains, looped earrings dangling from blondish long hair. I peeked over my orange frameless glasses with a rhinestone flower on the bottom of my left lens, trying to decide if this young woman at which I stared was sassy, hippie, or… hopeless.

I'd recently won the poise and appearance categories at Miss Junior Miss of Ohio, in Marietta, on the outskirts of Columbus. I was reigning Best Body at Liberty High School. Boys drove by the house more frequently now, some honking, some waving, some laughing, all blasting off into the dark night with a trace of exhaust smoke. When the phone rang, it was usually for me, and it was always a boy.

But my confidence on this night wavered. I was going it alone, a first. I had not seen Frankie Valli in two years. He was a star, and gorgeous, and I now faced the stark difference between the toy doll Frankie and the Frankie who would take the Stambaugh stage to thunderous adoration. I had to acknowledge that the April in the mirror had not turned out exactly like the April doll. I could not, tonight, bend and shape the two molded plastic figurines to my liking, order them to do my bidding.

I looked down from my closet door mirror at my bare feet, wiggled my carefully manicured toes, bursting with excitement over the impending adventure, but too nervous to get started. I tiptoed to reach the top shelf of my closet, pulled out the old purple Frankie hat, which I'd seemingly retired as of the last concert. Honestly, I did not know what I wanted or expected from this evening, and had not thought consciously about whether I wanted the reflected light of Frankie Valli's star, a dad to replace my own absent father, or something else entirely. In truth, I hardly thought about it, except to say that I knew it was vital to my very being that my relationship with Frankie—if that was what it was—continue, maybe even grow. Whatever it was that had allowed me entry, even in such small ways, to Frankie's world, had embedded itself into my self-image, and somehow the April that pal-ed around with Frankie Valli was infinitely preferable to an April with no celebrity connections.

I cradled that Frankie hat, set it delicately upon my perfectly manufactured head. I walked back to the mirror. I tried it with the sunglasses, then without. Posed with my hands on my hips, and without. I could almost, but not quite, see that six-year-old April, all innocence and enthusiasm, all joy and hope. I made the slow walk back to my closet, raised up on my bare feet, and returned it to the top shelf, relegating it to storage, like old pictures I'd rarely look at but needed to know were there: the picture of Dad playing his saxophone with the U.S. Army band; the picture of Dad and Mom at the Mount Carmel Church hall, standing by their wedding cake; the picture of them on their honeymoon in the Poconos; the picture of Mom and Dad with Grandma Kata and Bumpy at a Detroit Tigers game.

In my closet, below that top shelf, were shoes. Lots of shoes. Saddle shoes. Patent leather pumps, three-inch and five-inch. White tie-up tennis shoes. Flip flops in white, black, and pink. Gold heels. Mary Janes for school. Shoes lay helter-skelter in every nook and cranny; shoes tumbled against and on top of each other, like a pileup on an icy Footwear Highway; shoes toed each other for space; shoes sparkled and shimmied, vying for attention. All except my pageant shoes, which were in tightly sealed boxes to protect the fabric and dyes made to match my dresses. I looked one way then another, tossing shoes aside to get a look at others, finally chose a cream, stacked three-inch sandal that clasped at my ankle and gave me a taller, leaner look. I fluffed my breasts, nabbed lip-gloss across my lips, stared at the mirror for approval, or maybe answers.

Downstairs, in the living room, I asked, "How do I look?"

Mom said, "Great," but that was usual. She seemed distracted. Mom did numbing work, and when she was not working she was out having affairs—one after another after another. This led inevitably to fights with Les, real fights, blood-and-black-eye fights, and it also led to Les desperately trying to tame her, like a cowboy trying to break a stubborn bronco. She cried a lot, more than ever, and went to church a lot, more than ever. She cried in church. Mom rallied just enough to tend to Jeff and me. But her unhappiness, her bitterness, her fatigue infiltrated the house. Infiltrated me.

I looked at Mom, but when she looked back her eyes were fixed in the distance, as if I'd already gone.

I opened the heavy Nova door, threw my bag into the back seat, and shook my butt into place. I rolled the window down ever so slightly, not wanting to muss my hair or melt my makeup. My key chain, tangled with a white homemade pom-pom and a house key, dangled from the ignition switch, and I sat now, transfixed by all those keys to all those doors we never locked in

Liberty. I started the car.

Boots Bell from W.H.O.T. drummed out the sound of the engine's grumble and of a tinkling the car had picked up after I'd scraped a few curbs and trampled a big rock. All these years later, I don't remember for sure what was on my mind then. Not sex. Not at all. What I do remember is the feeling that I was embarking on something life altering, monumental. Maybe that was just the way 16-year-old April interpreted the world—if it was happening to me, it *must* be important. Maybe it was merely that this concert *was* different. I was alone, and if not a woman, a close facsimile thereof. Maybe it was some intuition that told me *this* was the end game, that all my striving, all my studying, all my primping... that I could actually *be* the person I pretended to be, once I believed it to be so.

At the stop sign at the end of my street, a big billboard advertised tonight's concert. Change had crept into and over Liberty, so gradual that the urban clutter seemed as natural now as the wide-open spaces had then. I continued down Fifth Avenue, checking myself in the rearview mirror like a new mom checking on her baby, making sure, making sure, making sure. I passed the tony tree-lined homes on my way into downtown, passed the spots where Grandma Kata and I had delivered eggs, but no more.

I navigated the immense, mostly empty parking lot, settled on a spot between two trucks. Sat there. It was not nearly dusk, and the sun reflected off my dingy gold hood, radiated from the hot tar. I drew a humid breath. Doors did not open for an hour, but for me this had already started. I got out of the car, slipped my keys into my straw bag, smiled. I shimmied and swayed toward the back of the building, all the way backstage, like a blind person navigating her own living room. I felt isolated, alone, and thought it odd how there were no barriers, no security, no managers. I paused and thought, briefly, how I had never done this without Aunt Ginny or Grandma Kata or at least my friends to guide me.

Men carried speakers, lights, back drops. Men zoomed here and there. Nothing but men—and me.

I knew this buzz: roadies, musicians, and "Oh, there is Bob Gaudio." He passed me with a glance. I walked up the wooden creaky steps toward the back of the stage and saw Frankie caressing the microphone, making little cooing sounds with his voice. I listened. I fell into a trance, and I must have closed my eyes because when they blinked open Frankie was looking my way, smiling.

I blushed. He moved toward me, not breaking eye contact. I could feel sweat trickling down my blouse. Frankie Valli. Frankie Valli! He was wearing a white silk shirt, tight white pants. He walked right up to me, within five inches of my face, and started to untangle the knot of chains covering my cleavage. He looked great, the way you would dream a rock star would look. I stammered in a tinny little voice, "Do you know who I am?"

He said, grinning with a boyish charm, "Hello, September."

September was Frankie's cute little play on my name April. Here we were, with inside jokes already. But while Frankie assumed I got my name from the month, I was actually named after the film *April Love*, in which characters played by Pat Boone and Shirley Jones fall in love on a Kentucky horse farm. Frankie didn't know that because, well, he basically didn't know anything about me. I didn't know anything about him. So how did the two of us, with so little to go on, wind up at this moment? I didn't know then what Frankie was thinking—though I have a good idea now—but I do know what I was thinking: "This is the man I'm going to marry."

All the trepidation of my life disappeared, and though I was still scared and surprised and uncertain, I was also exhilarated. I was confident, not in what would happen next, because I had no real thoughts on that, but on my purpose, namely: follow this man to wherever he takes me next.

There were, most certainly, more words exchanged—

small talk, probably. But I couldn't hear or process any of it. Finally, Frankie asked, "Do you want to sit backstage while I sing?" I suppose Frankie came off as arrogant to some, but his presumption that the world wanted to watch him, to hear him, was correct. He was alluring in every way—handsome, rich, sweet when he wanted to be. And above all, *that voice*. It was a gift, and I for one was unequipped to disentangle the music from the man.

I was 16, and this slick Frankie patter did not strike me as practiced, or routine, or anything other than a blessing. I did not do drugs, or smoke, or fornicate. I prayed and I pranced and I studied. But now, without knowing what was really happening, I had a vice, and my introduction to addiction felt, as I'm sure it's felt to gamblers and alcoholics and junkies before me, euphoric.

Standing in the shadows, looking out on the harsh powerful stage lights, the concert flashed by in seconds. It also lasted a lifetime. I listened and I sang, but I also obsessed over what would happen next. Should I fawn like a fan, or support like a friend? Was I Purple Hat April or Orange Hippie Glasses April? Did I speak or wait to be spoken to? I did not know what I wanted, nor did I know what Frankie wanted. But I already knew that whatever Frankie did or said, I would agree.

Backstage in the shadows, the music, the words, felt somehow more intimate. Frankie faced the crowd, he sang to the crowd. But viewed from the side, I heard and observed his seduction of the audience almost as a voyeur. Frankie's studied concentration gave a glimpse into his craftsmanship, especially on those high high notes that must have been easier for him to reach ten years ago when I first faced him as a little, almost-first grader. His sway and his eyes hinted at emotional attachment to the lyrics. His open-necked collar, with that tuft of velvety hair peeping out, belied a confidence in his sex appeal, and when he opened his eyes coming out of a stanza, those blues betrayed animal urges he knew were reciprocated. He was a different Frankie than the one I'd first encountered. The boyish good looks and meticulous sleek suits had given way to a groovier aura. His hair was fuller, his face lined with experience and memories, his body liberated. The band and stage setup were also now more eclectic, with a trio of black backup singers adding richness to the harmonies, and more pastoral backdrop colors enriching the senses. The stage lights popped psychedelic colors that came to me in a kind of second-hand *pow* that made the experience almost hallucinatory.

One of Frankie's people had scooted a chair over here in the wings, but I mostly stood until the end. The concert ended with "Can't Take My Eyes Off of You," at which point I sat, not knowing how to act, who to be. I watched Frankie but listened to the crowd. The intensity of the experience had reached a crescendo: "Ba-*da*-ba-*da*-ba-*da*-*da*-*da*-*da*-*da*-da…" Little female gasps and cries and shrieks escaped pretty little mouths as the music built toward a climax. "Oh pretty *baby*…"

Frankie and a few others scattered to my side of the stage while the other Four Seasons escaped to the other side. The auditorium was in an absolute frenzy, every single person on his or her feet, clapping wildly, stomping, hooting, and yelling, "Encore!"

Somebody threw Frankie a towel, he dabbed drivels of sweat from his forehead, and threw the towel back in the general direction of the stagehand. Frankie walked over to me, smiled, put his hand on my shoulder, and said, "Stay right here."

Frankie and the band returned to the stage to thunderous applause. The band kicked into "Bye, Bye, Baby." It was a party now, a party nobody wanted to end. If Frankie and the others had kept playing indefinitely, there would be stragglers still there today, gone grey and wrinkled and limp but still yelling for more.

Frankie again returned to my side, and this time said, "Just a few more minutes. Don't go anywhere."

The applause, the adulation, seemed enough almost to bring down Stambaugh Auditorium. Rafters literally shook. Then a tinkle, the beginnings of a melody, and the arena quieted. The musicians, nearly breathless now, roared to life, one last sprint to the finish line. The final number was "Let's Hang On," and Frankie sang it lovingly, from the heart, and as he did he stared into several thousand sets of eyes. Each girl in the audience stared back at Frankie, and each girl believed Frankie sang to just her. "Don't let go girl, we've got a lot…"

But I knew Frankie was singing to *me*.

The backstage group moved downstairs to the Green Room, where Frankie did live radio interviews with W.H.O.T. and other stations. There were people milling about, buzzing. Some were drinking, some were talking. Flirtation was the accepted mode of communication. There was excitement everywhere. Frankie kept holding up one finger toward me, "One second," as he completed his post-concert duties. Another index finger in my direction, "Hold on."

Then Frankie was working the room. He moved easily from one person to the next, meeting and greeting, hugging and kissing. Finally, I was the last stop on Frankie's lap around the Green Room. He looked right into my eyes, and I guess I looked right back. I'd been going over this moment in my head, pretty much since I'd left the house—long before, really—but I still had no answers. "Do you want to talk some more?" Frankie asked.

I assented, whether with a whispered "Yes," a nod of the head, or some primitive sign language, I can't say.

Frankie asked, "Do you know where the Holiday Inn is?"

I did. The Holiday Inn on Belmont Avenue technically had a Youngstown address, but it was just blocks from my home in Liberty. There was a nightlife scene in Youngstown, even in Liberty—rock bands rotated from one venue to another, and people migrated after work for certain happy hour specials. Holiday Inn was part of that scene, but of course I knew this only from talk. I was just 16.

"I'll meet you in a half hour," Frankie said, before giving me a soft kiss on the head. That kiss: it was fatherly and sensual, all at once. It meant something. "Do you know how to get there? You okay to get out of here?"

It was just now that I realized I was about to sleep with Frankie Valli. And even then, I couldn't be too sure that this wouldn't all fall apart, through some social screw-up, or my vast ignorance, or plain bad luck. I wanted this now. I was ready.

The Nova drove itself, and I parked way back in the Holiday Inn lot, embarrassed, a bit, that my car did not meet rock star standards; that nothing I owned, or did, nothing of who I was, qualified for whatever it was that came next. Soon I was standing in the lounge, scanning the booths and bar. A comedian cracked jokes to a handful of hearty chuckles, but most everybody ignored the act on stage and conversed in normal barroom tones, not even a pretense of politeness to the performer.

The Holiday Inn bar was enormous, and heads bobbed in animated conversation. It was mostly men, and among them I recognized band and crew members, guys like Tom DeVito, Joey Long, other guys I recognized but didn't know what they did. The doorman did not card me—then or ever, anywhere. Attractive women, it seemed, got a pass.

It was dark, and loud, but through the darkness, through the noise, I spotted Frankie. He waved me over to a booth populated with this guy and that. Frankie acknowledged them—seven or eight guys—as they disengaged, migrating away from the booth and toward the bar, as if they'd received a secret signal. The last one to leave—one of the Four Seasons band members—nodded to Frankie, and Frankie said, "Early night tonight." He laughed, said, "Yeah?"

Frankie smirked and said, "Maybe I'll see you back down here. One, maybe."

Then it was just the two of us. Me and Frankie Valli.

Frankie drank something I never heard of before; I ordered a Bacardi and Coke like I had seen my Aunt Ginny order, and soon the waitress plopped it in front of me. I sipped from a straw then moved the straw aside and drank in bigger gulps. What we talked about, I cannot say. The room absolutely rotated. It surged and rescinded. I remember Frankie talking to me not as a child, exactly, but not as an adult either. He was the older camp counselor, clearly wiser, obviously in charge, but also a conspirator. He brushed my hand, searched my eyes. This was 1974, and decorum differed enormously from now. There were, of course, no cell phone selfies, but neither were there autograph hounds or giggly groupies or random admirers stopping to sing Frankie's praises. We were left alone.

All these years later, I can see how, for Frankie, it was another in a long line of post-concert unwinding sessions: a so-so night at the Holiday Inn lounge in which the floor show failed to interest and the boys in the band would wait. Bedding a teenage girl was stress relief, or maybe a perk of the life, perhaps even just part of the routine. For me, though, this was romance such as I'd never experienced, a peek into the crystal ball that was adulthood, a prelude not to sex but to a kind of life in which adventure and respect and adulation filled the hours and days and weeks and years. The whole scene—for I was part of it now—did not appear to me in grays and blacks, but rather in oranges and purples. Everything was vivid. Everything was important. Everything was magic.

Finally, after what seemed a lifetime, but was probably all of 20 minutes, Frankie asked, "Do you want to go up to my room so we can be alone?"

I said, or maybe uttered is more accurate, "Uh-huh."

Frankie orchestrated the whole thing. He turned on some music, poured me another drink, then kissed me, long and passionately. Our first kiss. I wasn't yet a drinker, hardly at all, and so the first rum drink, not to mention the kiss, already had me in a sort of dream state. I was wet. I was hungry. I was scared. Frankie poured his own drink, stirred it with his finger.

"I'm going to the restroom," he said. "Get undressed and get into bed."

The bathroom door closed and I did not hesitate. All was clear now—well, maybe not all, but enough of all. I was so nervous. I whipped my clothes down on the floor and jumped into bed, pulling the covers up. The cold reminded me that I had absolutely nothing on between the covers and me.

I lay there, snuggling, the bed warming. Then the bathroom door opened.

Frankie emerged from the bathroom naked. I lay in the bed, thinking, "Holy Shit!" His uncircumcised penis dangled, like a homemade ornament. Of course, I'd never seen any penis, circumcised or not, so to me this was just a penis. Frankie's penis. I knew Frankie was short—I was short, too—but from that moment on I never considered him a little man. Without clothes, standing unadorned, flogging his appendage back and forth, he somehow seemed heroic. Frankie tucked himself into the bed next to me. The lights were dim, and we lay there, both naked, kissing and petting, petting and kissing, all the while Frankie explaining to me what was going to happen next. "It might hurt a little at first, but it's alright, it's good," he said.

He said, "There might be some blood."

I knew there wouldn't be, since I'd broken my cherry twirling baton. But the rest I was just guessing at. In some ways, this felt like a training session—Frankie carefully giving me advice that would be handy for now and the future. It should have signaled to me that there would be more to come, that this wasn't a one-night stand, but I'd not even considered such things. To me, this was love. Clearly, as Frankie crawled on top of me and used his hand to guide his penis inside me, we were both feeling it. He came in a matter of a few minutes; I did not. Then Frankie rolled off me, held me for a lengthy squeeze. He retreated to the bathroom.

I felt the ooze between my legs, and thought briefly of the fact that I was not on birth control. Like a flash, I remembered my baby sister. I mostly didn't remember I'd ever had a baby sister. I suppose I'd buried the thought deep in my subconscious. It was a few years before I'd first met Frankie, after Mom had divorced Dad but before she'd married Les. There was a woman, Mary Jane, to whom Les was still married. When Mom delivered his baby she took it over to Grandma Kata's. It was a row.

Aunt Ginny screamed, "I'm already raising your one daughter, I *will not* raise another!"

Grandma Kata said, "I will only have one of your children over here. You have to choose: April or Suzette." That was my sister's name, Suzette. So we drove to Niles, Ohio, a silent ride except for Suzette's cute and awful screeches, her sad-happy purrs. Mom gave up the baby to a woman we never saw again. We never saw Suzette again, either, the only reminder being Mom's annual bout of depression around her birthday in July.

I didn't want to be like that: a reckless girl who had unwanted pregnancies and a storehouse of regret. But my anxiety and horror passed in the same flash: Frankie was in charge, and surely Frankie would not let anything bad happen. Frankie returned, still naked, now limp again, and said, "Now you go to bathroom, then we'll go back in the bed and talk."

I wrapped a sheet around myself before getting out of bed. In the bathroom, I wiped between my legs with a hand towel, peed in the toilet, lingered a second at the mirror. When I returned, Frankie lay in the bed, smoking, and I nestled beside him, leaning on his shoulder. He said, "Don't go doing this with everybody; you don't do this with everybody."

He needn't have told me. Of course I wouldn't do this with anybody else. How could I? My blondish hair sprawled across his matted dark chest. I felt awkward and confident, restless and contented. I knew, then, that this was the beginning of our life together, me and Frankie, Frankie and me, not knowing or even imagining that Frankie already had a little blonde girl for a wife, just three years older than myself, waiting for him somewhere in New Jersey. She was undoubtedly wiser to his ways than I, wiser to the ways of the world.

Frankie said, "It's getting late, I don't want you to be too late. I've got to get some rest."

"Are we going to see each other again?" I asked.

Frankie had turned 40 that year. He was older than most of my schoolteachers, older than my dance and baton instructors, older than the Hollywood idols on TV. He was 24 years older than me, the little farm girl enjoying her Sweet 16 year.

"Yeah, we'll find each other," he said.

Frankie gave me his manager's phone number, and I declined his offer to walk me to my car. Soon I was tiptoeing back into my house. Before I could open my bedroom door, Mom called out, "April, you home?"

"Yeah, Mom."

"Did you have a good time?"

"Yeah, Mom."

The lights in my bedroom were off, and morning would be on me in a hurry. But I couldn't sleep. *Mrs. Valli.*

*Mrs. April Valli.*

*Wife of Frankie Valli.*

I felt a little like Cinderella returning from the ball, with one exception: I knew there would be more balls.

*April and Mom at Conneaut Lake Park in Jamestown, PA.*

# THE ROAD TO THE ROAD

"Your birth control script is filled?"

"Yes, Mom."

We were driving toward Canton. Frankie had said he wasn't coming to Youngstown on this tour. Instead he invited me to meet up with his tour bus and ride along. For how long, he didn't say; for how long, I didn't ask.

Mom was not very inquisitive, either. She had suggestions more than questions, suggestions like, "Don't say anything to anybody about this. This is private. You like Frankie, and it's none of anybody's business."

Mom, like me, was content to let somebody else drive the bus.

Mom guided her new white Pontiac based on directions I'd scribbled in an old homework notebook. I was nervous. I tried to imagine life on the road with a rock band, and mostly when I did, I saw glamour and excitement. But my anticipation amounted to an uneasy thrill, like a roller coaster chugging toward its pinnacle before the free fall. I knew now that sex would be a big part of it. Whatever purity of mind and body I'd possessed a month prior was now gone, a condition to which I could never return, not even for a visit. Plus, I was 16—hormonal, hot, bothered. I wanted this, too, maybe as much as Frankie, maybe more. But who knew? I was not privy to Frankie's thoughts. He was still if not the father figure, then the older camp counselor, and he'd been cast in the role of sage conspirator, the mastermind who at once abetted my deviousness and promised to keep me out of trouble.

The Ohio landscape pinged green at this high point of summer. Corn stalks shot up in perfectly symmetrical fields. Farm stands advertised their wares. Cows lazed in the fields, and the occasional brood of chickens could be spotted running about. The lambs were already getting big, weaned from their mothers and discovering the world, some of them destined, without their knowledge, to become chops, while others would be granted a lifetime of having their teats firmly milked.

I glanced over at Mom. Her grip was loose on the steering wheel. I had long since given up on Mom directing my life, but I wished now for something, anything, helpful. Her bobbed hair and A-line dress lent her a certain elegance—she was still a beauty—and her small heels pressed lightly on the accelerator. I knew there was a big drop from the image Mom projected and the life she lived, but as long as she could continue to hit the gas, and do so with those alluring ankles, I guess to the world she was doing just fine.

"Can you get a ride to Canton and we'll hang around for a while?" is how Frankie had put the proposition, meaning, I suppose, that we'd screw our way across country, and along the way experience whatever joy and beauty and excitement came our way. I wanted to ask Mom about the sex part. In this arena, surely, she was an expert. The whole of my experience had been the brief Holiday Inn romp, and I fidgeted now thinking of all the sexual adventures I had *not* had. But even then, I was guilty of projecting all my passion on the giving, not the receiving. I wondered what I should or could do to make Frankie happy.

Looking back, I wish I'd been focused on myself. I wish I would have daydreamed about how to spread my legs just so when Frankie bowed his head to me; fantasized about pushing Frankie down and straddling him so I'd feel him deep inside. I should have wondered what it would be like to grip the headboard and be penetrated from behind; mused about the thrill of having my toes and neck and small of my back licked; debated the merits of having red wine and strawberries while Frankie teased my erogenous zones; contemplated foreplay in saunas and showers. I wish I would have imagined romantic possibilities, like intimate candlelit dinners, and hand holding in a darkened theater, and walks around my hometown at sunrise. I should have been thinking about the inextricable tangle of love and trust and security that informs great sex. But: no. I was thinking of the best way to give Frankie a blowjob.

I'd never administered oral sex, though I knew about it, somehow, the way one just knows about things. TV, maybe. But this was the 70s, pre-cable, pre-Internet, so my notions were based on cutaways in which no mouth ever met an actual penis. Even language, such as euphemisms for body parts and sexual acts, were strictly forbidden, and saying *words*, much less performing *acts*, was considered vulgar and something akin to perverted. I was also tempered by a religious upbringing in which premarital sex was a sin, and my role as a woman was to serve my man and essentially procreate. So... did I lick or suck? Did I lick *and* suck? What about the testicles? Did I squeeze, lick, kiss? All of the above? My imagination, at this point, was limited, and I failed to think of other ways to please Frankie. A hummer, though: I knew men wanted that. Step one, then: give Frankie a blowjob that would make me indispensable.

"Mom?"

She seemed far away. I followed her gaze to an old barn with rotted roof and peeled red paint, an old barn with gaps between the wood, an old barn surely in disuse for years, but which had somehow evaded the wrecking ball. As we zoomed past the barn, I wondered whether some farmer had consciously decided to let Mother Nature take its course, or if that farmer had just been too lazy to confront the barn's mortality.

"Miss April Lynn," she murmured.

"Nothing," I said.

Make no mistake: for me, this was about love. My obsessive thoughts about sex were an acknowledgement that I couldn't have what I wanted without giving Frankie what he wanted. I was sure it would eventually be about love for Frankie, too. But not if I couldn't blow his mind, which is to say, blow *him*. What happened then? I only had a sense, no more than that, of the intricacies of a male orgasm. Sperm was milky, I knew that, but not milk, not exactly. How would it taste? Was I supposed to swallow? Was there a lot of it, or just a little squirt? If I didn't swallow, wouldn't that be messy? If I did swallow, wouldn't my mouth then taste and smell like sperm? It did not occur to me to question whether I would like this; that wasn't the point. The point was: I needed to do this in such a perfect way that Frankie would be addicted.

Perfection was something I knew from majorette camp. I'd go down to Marietta, Ohio, in the summer to lead our crew. If you were in my line, you needed to stand taller, suck in your stomach, do it again. Addiction was something I knew from my family. Alcohol. Sex. Gambling. Pills. Once you had to have something, you would stop at nothing to get it.

The countryside turned urban, or at least relatively so, and soon Mom said, "We're here."

It was a Holiday Inn. Again, a Holiday Inn. A huge unmarked brown and beige bus idled in the parking lot. No glamour, no glitz, just… plain. I fluffed and flipped my hair, pushed up my orange-tinted glasses, the heart-shaped stones rising to meet the sun. Here I was, in my Orange Phase, a nearly grown woman, or so I thought, shrugging off my old piousness and embracing the psychedelic seventies, about to embark on a road trip as a rock star's chosen lady.

Yet, for part of me, my Pink Phase persisted. I felt sweat under my armpits as I saw flashes of April and Frankie dolls in little traveling cases; heat on my thighs as I thought about walking across my old bedroom with books atop my head; dampness on my forehead as I remembered girlfriends on the block coming over to play. Then, I would have said that all those youthful experiences were training for here, for now, but in retrospect I think my brain was reminding me that my bond with Cute-Little-Me April was stronger than my bond with Sexpot April.

Still, there was no doubt that, physically, I'd changed, that I'd left childhood behind, and my hard nipples stood, or pinged, as testament to that. I tipped forward on my high wedge sandals as I opened the car door, raced to the trunk, suddenly sure I was holding up the band, holding up the tour, an immediate source of irritation for the whole entourage. I pulled out my suitcase and noticed that Mom had left her purse in the car, meaning she would not stay longer than the time it took to hand me off.

And to whom was Mom handing me off?

I tap, tap, tapped on the closed bus door, an enormous steel barrier between *this* and *that*, between what was and what would be. Mom stood behind me. Joe Long cracked the door open, held up a single finger, and in a kindly growl yelled back, "April's here."

No more "The Hat," no more "The Girl from Youngstown." I was April now, real and defined and soon to be inside looking out, rather than outside looking in.

Mom smiled, whispered, "Are you ok?"

I nodded. I straightened my fringed belt, which had slid askew around my hips. It was then, in the brief interval at which

I awaited, entranced, that I thought about going home. Just a fleeting thought, a thought of safety; and then, in the place of those doubts, there was Frankie.

He was dressed casually—jeans and an open-collared shirt—but still looked utterly perfect. He was a tiny man, but as he came to the door, he looked down at me from the height of four bus steps. There was an intensity to the way he looked first into my eyes, and then moved his gaze down to my mother. He held out a hand to lift me onto the bus, into his world, and as he did so, he bent down and politely kissed my cheek. He turned to Mom, introduced himself with that Jersey accent, and made a rash of compliments about what a lovely person she must be to raise such a special girl, about her own appearance, about her charm. Basically, Frankie said all the things Mom wanted to hear. I listened—I was on the top step now, equal with Frankie—and heard in his voice a certain exoticness, like there were endless stories he could tell, lessons he could teach. I rotated my shoulder so that now it was Frankie and I looking down at Mom, and though I felt independent, I realized I was waiting for her final approval.

She said to Frankie, "Take care of April," then to me, "Call," and she dismissed herself, just a pretty head bobbing across a near-empty stretch of asphalt in the shadows of a Holiday Inn sign whose neon would not activate until much later.

*April with Mom, wearing her Millers Towing sash before a pageant in Ohio.*

# THE ROAD TO MY FUTURE

The motor started. I had no guidebook for this, for how to be a pop star's girlfriend, for how to act on an hours-long drive with a hoard of male musicians, for what to say to adults at least a generation older than myself.

I was seated at a round snack table, with Bob, Tom, and Joe perched on the other cushions. Frankie introduced me around, saw that my bags were stowed. Bobby asked, "What kind of music do you like?" to which I replied, "Jazz." It was a blatant lie—I knew nothing whatsoever about jazz—and I don't know what motivated me to tell it, except to say that I was unconsciously trying to determine who I was supposed to be. Forget about who I was, because I hardly knew. I fielded other polite questions, but largely The Four Seasons and entourage seemed barely interested in me.

All the while, we were rolling toward Flint, Michigan, the next stop on the tour. It was about six or seven hours to there, six or seven hours of what I could only presume would be continuing awkwardness. "Why don't you ever write a song about April?" I asked.

One of them said, "Nothing rhymes with April."

*Hold still, April?*

*Get your fill, April?*

*All the frills of Ap-ril?*

*Un-til, Ap-ril?*

*What a thrill, my April?*

"I guess you're right," I said.

Frankie was off somewhere up front in the bus, and now I wondered whether I was totally on my own here or whether Frankie would be my guide or chaperone or what. My stomach gurgled. I glanced toward the bathroom, thinking, "Oh, God, I'm going to have to crap *here*." I was still thinking about that inevitable blowjob, only now, as I looked around, I was thinking about that blowjob on a bus—surely that would add a level of difficulty. I still had not determined whether to suck or lick, swallow or spit, whether to approach Frankie's from my knees or upside down. On the bus, though? That seemed more like a circus trick, and I convinced myself that sex would wait until the next stop, when we were settled into a hotel in Flint.

The band drifted into other talk, such that I was there, but not there. I daydreamed about being home, listening to Frankie on my record player, and for a hot moment it occurred to me that that was preferable to this.

I was lonely.

The bus eased off the highway and into a McDonald's parking lot, the engine sighing to a stop. The band gang tackled the counter while Frankie found me and duly turned, again, into my escort. "You hungry?" he asked. I nodded.

We walked hand-in-hand into the McDonald's. At that moment, I not only felt Frankie's sweetness but also gratitude for his attention, and that gratitude quickly turned to something like lust as I watched the way he charmed the cashier, the way he bit his lip, the way he smooshed his fries between his burger, the way he focused on my words, sparse though they were.

Suddenly, I did want to kiss Frankie, and right there in McDonald's for everyone to see. The bus driver waved us back to the bus, and Frankie helped me up those steep steps, just as he'd picked me up on stage as a little girl. He whispered, "You tired?"

"Yes," I said, "Exhausted. I was up early."

"Good," he said. He cupped my chin with one hand, touched my nose with his other finger. "Let's lie down a while."

We had our own space, as it were, on a bottom bunk, with burlap-type drapery wrapped around us. Bunk beds were arranged throughout the bus. These were our sleeping quarters, our only shot at privacy, if you didn't count the bathroom. I glanced around. The other guys were in their bunks, reading, flipping cards, working a puzzle, and generally making like they weren't spectators to our impending tryst, though of course they were. Their bunks might as well have been bleachers, and our bunk the playing field.

The blankets were brown and the space small, just a box around a twin bed. There was enough room for the two of us, no more. As a 16-year-old girl, I was on the fringes of a world in which young lovers stole off to basement corners, or hunted for an unoccupied bedroom, or inclined car seats, or found a lonely wooded area. This—rock tour or no—was much the same.

Still, I was wet with anticipation. Nervous, self-conscious, ashamed, worried, all of that. But dripping wet. My inner thighs were stuck to my tight-fitting jeans, so when Frankie said, "Take your clothes off," it was like a game show challenge. I unclasped the ankle straps on my sandals, plopped on my back, wriggled my jeans down to my ankles. I lifted my shirt over my head, but left on my bra. Just like high school, this would be quick—no time for candlelight, conversation, and foreplay. I made like a roly poly, knees to my chest as I tugged my jeans to the floor, and then slid my white cotton panties to my toes before dropping them.

I was sweating. Frankie was getting undressed and sliding under the covers next to me. Now for that blowjob.

Only… it didn't happen, not this time. I squeezed his thing, honked it like a horn, really, and then he was aroused, and then he was on top of me. He poked and I pushed, and I tried to be very quiet, but Frankie's heavy breathing and tiny moans sounded, to me, like a helicopter landing. But I was in no position to shush or stop. We bucked to the rhythms of Interstate 80, hitting the occasional pothole as we purred toward climax. He came inside me. I did not come.

I was flushed and hot. He'd started on top, but finished with me on my side, all kinds of poking and prodding, slipping and sliding, until, *poof*. Details of the gymnastics that allowed us to maneuver into a new position were lost, like how you're walking, walking, walking, and when you look up, you're there, without any memory of the individual steps you took on the way. He kissed me gently and told me to roll over. "Doll, get some rest. I'm getting up."

I didn't know enough to be unsatisfied. The Women's Liberation movement was charging through America in 1974, but it detoured around Liberty, Ohio. Sure, we had women earning good money at General Electric. Yes, divorces were rampant. There were even businesswomen, like Grandma Kata. But the era of free love, bra burning, key parties, open marriages, and other sexually liberating practices was kept away by our working class, church-going roots. Men were still dominant, women passive, at least in most relationships. I made no demands for my own pleasure—it never even occurred to me. Partly, this was because of the age and power gap between Frankie and me. But mostly, it was who I was, who I would be. I'll never know if I'd have learned to be more selfish, or at least self-aware, had I started my sexual adventures with a boy my own age. Perhaps, had I considered my own erogenous needs, I would have better pleased Frankie, maybe even become a full partner in this relationship. Instead, I scooched away from the wet spot on the sheets, a wet spot of my own making, too young and too embarrassed and too awkward to at least discreetly finish the job myself.

The makeshift curtains, hung on a pole like shower curtains, suddenly became my protection against the social tragedy that awaited me in the bus. No way was I going out there to face the Four Seasons—I wouldn't even have the luxury of a walk of shame, because there was no place to which I could escape.

What I knew, but I was sure the Four Seasons did not, was how deep and true my love for Frankie really was. I figured they would discover this over time, but for now, I just eyed the wet spot and wondered how long it would take to dry, considering there did not appear to be much in the way of full-service laundry at our disposal.

At The Hilton, in Flint, Michigan, our pattern was established. The bus would pull up usually a handful of hours ahead of when we needed to get to the concert hall. We were all weary from the road, but Frankie was horny. He liked to have intercourse straight away, nap, and then transition to a kind of seriousness in preparation for the evening's performance. We'd ride in a limo to the venue, and it was upon arrival that we'd get the rock star treatment. I say *we* because I was treated as part of the famous entourage. People spotted the limo and came to it—not the screaming throngs like you see in old Beatles clips, but a small band of devotees. Then there would be the concert. Then the Green Room interviews and post-concert party, including women the band members had picked out as potential late-night partners. Then onto the hotel bar, where these new or renewed relationships would be accelerated with the help of open bar tabs and conveniently located hotel rooms.

In Flint, I experienced several firsts. I kissed Frankie gently on his neck, and worked my way down his hairy chest, to his navel, and finally my lips arrived on his penis. I used my tongue, my lips, my breathe, my hands, and then Frankie bobbled my head like a toy giveaway, all the while offering encouragement like a Little League coach—"That's it, April," "Right there is good," "You got the hang of this"—until he exploded. I was vaguely aware of my own power then, my tongue, my lips, my hot breath driving Frankie into a frenzied excitement that I and I alone controlled to the end. I decided to swallow, but when the gusher went off, the velocity took me a bit off guard, and I inadvertently closed my eyes and my mouth. Frankie's load splattered my eyes and mouth and chin, such that my face became a canvas for a kind of creamy Jackson Pollock painting. The little bit that made it into my mouth was salty and not terrible tasting, medicine that you feared more than it merited.

I also signed my first autograph. Stepping out of the limo at that first concert, a young fan waved me over and excitedly asked, "Are you with Frankie?" I signed, and as I did, somebody snapped my photo. I still had no idea Frankie was married, and still had no instructions to be secretive. It felt like I was Frankie's girlfriend, or at least, moving toward that status.

For a moment that lingered maybe two decades too long, I felt not like a star's plaything, but like… a star.

Only one day into the road trip, home already seemed distant and somehow detached from my life. Back there, I was entering that critical transition period. As a junior, I would begin a two-year cycle in which all my major activities would be showcased at the varsity (high-profile) level, before plopping into the mental archives, turning into yearbook fodder, the kind of stuff we'd laugh about at reunions. For almost everyone like me, our youthful ambitions become bait. We cast our résumés far and wide in hopes of being accepted into good colleges and then landing a good job. I was too short to model, I was told. At five-foot-two, I needed to grow another six to ten inches in order to compete for a real career, and that was not going to happen. I wasn't even tall enough to be a stewardess.

This road trip, this blossoming love affair with Frankie Valli, was my way to avoid the grind and capture the glitter. I didn't so much think this as feel it. There was a change in the way I was perceived that I wanted to make permanent.

*April and Frankie.*

# THE LIFE

It was not a whirlwind of debauchery, not the drug- and sex-crazed almost-hallucination you see in so many rock dramas and rockumentaries. Not for me, anyway. The band members and roadies and hangers on did coke, smoked pot, drank heavily, and certainly the number of groupies popping up and disappearing rivaled a game of Whack-A-Mole. There was all of that, though it was much more subdued than Hollywood would have you believe. Frankie and the Four Seasons and everybody else affiliated with the band seemed highly interested in the perks. They maneuvered to get the perks. But they cherished their careers and their music above all else—essentially, they had jobs, and they worked in the sex and drugs (which had become so routine as to bore many of them) around their real schedules. Plus, I was insulated from the rock scene, probably because Frankie was aware that I was, at best, a young woman. More truthfully, I was just a girl. He would sprinkle fatherly advice like, "Don't ever do drugs," and

"You have to go to college," and, "This isn't something you should be doing with everybody" in between our own romping sessions, which became increasingly pleasurable for me.

I managed somehow to ignore or miss all the clear signals that this was fantasy, or something like vacation, and that the hard realities that were my real life waited patiently back home, where I belonged. Frankie and I breakfasted together; we limoed over to sound checks; we lazed around the hotel lobby with the other Seasons; we had nice dinners at good restaurants; we listened to music in bars. I wanted to believe we were in love, and Frankie, like many womanizers I met later in life, was good at leading me there. He had a way of making me the focus of his intense attention, if only for a short while, so that in those moments I felt trust, admiration, affection, and intimacy. I knew *I* was in love.

But our time together was always brief, even on this concert tour where I was a constant fixture in the entourage. Frankie would gently transition away from me with soft statements like, "I have to go downstairs to make a call," or, "I need to get my rest," or, "You stay here."

Frankie did not say I was his girlfriend, nor did he ever say he was single. I suppose he didn't care enough one way or another to dispel the myths I was creating. He wanted me on some level, that I knew, but in my young imagination, there was a world of possibility ahead that Frankie never even entertained. For me, the tour bus wheels spun across a beautiful rhinestone path that led to a place in which I was inextricably a part of Frankie's life, *this* life. Frankie was famous. I, in my own way, was famous, a glimmer of which I'd experienced when reporters had asked if I'd agree to an interview. We were living a famous life, a free life, a beautiful and exciting life, and surely there must be a way to make this go on and on and on.

That first hotel lobby in Flint set the tone for the trip. It was gorgeous, but more than that it was extravagant. Over the top.

The enormous crystal chandeliers, the marble floor, the velvet chairs with velvet buttons—it all screamed wealth, success, *we made it!*

Frankie and I, the band, the roadies, the managers—we all glided through the Hilton like we owned it, or rather, like it existed all for us. There was an indoor pool; a gym with every conceivable piece of equipment; a concierge, something I'd never heard of, whose job it was to basically make our lives better, easier, more exciting, and efficient; and three restaurants I imagined were like the ones in Las Vegas. Did Frankie have a concert in Vegas anytime soon? I wanted to go, to see it all. This, it seemed, was living, and only briefly did I wonder how long this tour would last; only briefly did I picture myself compiling lists of "reach" and "safe" colleges, or grinding away at SAT prep work, or twirling a baton in a tiny, sweaty gymnasium, or sitting down at a high school guidance counselor's desk to explore future careers. Was I predisposed to a career in nursing, or better suited to the life of a grammar school teacher? All of that was just a month or so away, but *now* seemed all that mattered, and *later*, in my mind, had been all but canceled.

After that, it was another Holiday Inn, but we remained in a Hilton state of mind, like switching to Korbel after downing some Dom Pérignon—it was the stuff you got drunk on that made the lasting impression.

In truth, the glamour and glitz was just the backdrop—we were so busy hustling from one concert to the next that there was no time to swim in the pool, work out in the gym, or admire any of the fancy touches. It was as though what mattered was that the amenities were there, not that we use them. We wanted to be set in a world fully designed to make us happy. We needed it. This was the life.

The trip swished and swooshed like the scenes in a View-Master. Hilton, swish, Holiday Inn. Flint, swoosh, Toledo. Front Row Theatre, swish, Cleveland State Theatre.

There were no wives on the road, and I thought about that some. I hadn't quite learned how, in the rock life, home was for family and the road for girlfriends. I didn't realize that, from the time you stepped onto the bus, through to the interviews in which you projected a kind of brand, through to the concerts where you were to the audience who they wanted you to be, and onto the parties at which you played the conquering heroes, that this entire scene was made up. I hadn't learned that our jobs were to merge the lines between the roles we played and who we really were.

If I were permitted the chance to give advice to my younger self, I would have told that April to be honest with herself. To reflect. To know the difference between words and actions. I'd say, "April, it's all there for you to see."

But I did not see.

In Michigan, we were at the hotel bar after the concert, everybody feeling good about themselves, the crinkle of sex in the air. I momentarily overcame my shyness to make a little joke, and it got laughs, and Frankie kissed me on the head and said, "Ain't she great?" That little morsel, and other morsels like it, filled me up. I misunderstood crumbs as the entrée. In my ignorance, I felt full.

We roamed the Midwest like a couple, but in the solitude of our bedroom or a rare quiet moment at a restaurant, Frankie acted the father. "You should go to college, April." "Don't get too close to these kinds of guys." "Sometimes it's easier to be a big fish in a small pond." "Always stay beautiful." "It's hard out there."

After sex was when things became less comfortable, maybe because that was when they were most comfortable. I was 16, and at that age—hell, at any age since—I interpreted sex as love. Here we were, two people, completely naked, on our knees, licking and teasing, spreading and thrusting, panting and moaning. We were out to please each other, to please ourselves, and in the satisfactory post-orgasm silence, the sweat would dampen my cleavage, the moisture would soak the sheets, my tangled hair would splay across the bed, and I would want clarity. "Are we going to see each other again?" "What's going on with us?" "Can you tell me how I can get a hold of you so we can stay in touch?"

Frankie was never dismissive, but he was masterful at getting to the other end of these discussions. He'd say, "We're having a great time, aren't we? I'm sure you and I will see each other again. You're adorable." I felt powerless and feared that to push would potentially upset whatever it was we had. Momentary appeasement was enough, and only later, typically as I pulsated with post-coital euphoria, would I want to nudge Frankie for something like a promise.

At the next concert venue, I was there first, waiting along with a good portion of the entourage, when Frankie walked into the room. I snuck glances at the band members, the roadies, the managers. As Frankie spoke, there was some combination of fear and admiration in their eyes. They were at Frankie's beck and call. I asked myself, then, "How do you get people to do whatever you want them to do?"

I had no answers, certainly not regarding Frankie.

I called Mom just twice from the road, and our conversations were that of a daughter checking in from summer camp. "You having a good time?" Mom asked. "Everything all right?" I had to call Mom at four p.m., after she was home from Packard Electric but before Les got home. Les didn't know anything about my trip.

Frankie's own eyes were hypnotic, and his gentlemanly ways seductive. He would allow me a Bacardi and Coke, but just one. He never swore around me. He held his arm out so I could loop mine inside. He opened doors for me.

Then one day, about ten days into it, Frankie said, "I think it's time for you to go home." He had already arranged a ride to the airport and booked my flight, so it was not a discussion. Frankie mentioned that he would be playing Hawaii in the near future. "Maybe you'll go to that one," he said.

As the airplane taxied on the runway at the Detroit Metropolitan Airport, I leaned my head back and fell into a deep sleep. For the first time since I'd left, I dreamt of Ohio, and when I woke, disoriented and literally flying through the clouds, I thought, "I'm almost home."

*April the aspiring model.*

# DANCING WITHOUT THE STAR

The checkered daylight lent Grandma Kata's farm a picture puzzle look, and as I gazed across sunlight, shade, sunlight, shade, I saw patterns. Depending on which way I tilted my head, I saw Dalmatian dogs, and British flags, and Indian heads, and ballerina slippers. I was wearing a celadon sheer blouse with a matching bra, an illusion of nothingness with which I'd become comfortable. I dabbed harlequin lipstick onto my lips with warm, green-yellow fingernails. I was now in my Green Phase, which coincided with my new All-Grown-Up-April Phase.

I was out at Grandma Kata's waiting for night, out in the still country air, far from Mom's hisses and Les's growls. Mom was heartbroken over the recent transfer to Texas of one of her boyfriend Bills. At home, she played "Unforgettable" and "Me and Mrs. Jones" over and over on a cassette tape. Les resented her sorrow, Mom resented his resentment, and the two brawled openly.

The world seemed so inconceivably big, and I fretted about how to wrangle it, to make it my own. My instinct, already forming, was to seize upon a single idea or plan, and to obsess about it. In my mind, if I could have that one thing, I would have it all. And I seized upon Frankie as the object that would fulfill all my desires.

"Helpless" is too weak a word for my condition. I had no access to Frankie Valli except on his terms, and the fact that I'd developed a fierce loyalty to our relationship made me vulnerable and anxious. My loyalty was misplaced, of course, but on this Saturday afternoon in the fall of 1975, I did not believe that.

What I did believe, still, against mounting evidence, was that Frankie and I would be married.

Mom had decided I would go to Oral Roberts Bible College in Tulsa, Oklahoma, upon graduation from Liberty High School. At the same time, she'd chosen "clerical" rather than "college prep" as my high school concentration, a course that was incompatible with my plans to study radio/TV communications, and that my guidance counselor discouraged.

"You'll always use those skills," was Mom's reasoning.

The clerical kids took basic accounting, business English, shorthand, and typing. We were learning secretarial and life skills, in preparation for a vocation and a life serving our male superiors, in some cases our would-be bosses, in most cases our future husbands. There were only girls in my classes, many of whom had already picked out their spouses or were intent on finding them. I thought of myself as so unlike my clerical classmates. I didn't see my I'm-Going-to-Marry-Frankie obsession as in any way equivocal to their I'm-Going-to-Marry-My-High-School-Sweetheart obsessions.

My visions of grandeur were not all my own. At home, I was still treated as a future star, the person in my family who would go on to be *Somebody* and lift us all up. Star of *what*, nobody knew.

We were going dancing, and I looked forward to an all-night romp down The Strip in Niles. I thought of myself as wild because I had started to tour the clubs with my older aunt and her boyfriend, because I sipped Diet Coke and Vodka, because I stayed out late, because I flirted. But in reality, my oat sewing was tame.

We converged at Alberini's, the first stop. I parked my gold 1970 Chevy Nova on 224th Street. Big Chuck's green vintage MG had beaten me there. My cousin Kathy's blue Mustang was there, too. Nobody at Alberini's carded at the door—they never did.

Inside, it was loud, and the lights were psychedelic and the mood celebratory. My greatest joy was to dance, uninhibited and inspired, in a way that I already knew incited men to impure thoughts. I had my own impure thoughts, but I compartmentalized them—dancing, for me, was not about sex, even if it appeared that way to the drunken horny men forming a perimeter around my show.

I was all dressed up. I twirled, soft and sensual, pulling my hair and letting it fall. I stroked my face with my hand, and then let my hand drop to my chest and caress my thighs. I had always danced erotically. It came so naturally I sometimes thought I might have been a burlesque star in a previous life. Even at four years old, Mom would take caution to put me in a full skirt when she knew there would be dancing, for example, at a wedding. You could call me a tease, and I guess I was, but I found joy in moving about the dance floor, feeling the music, glimpsing the hunger of the men. I was just coming to understand the great power that came with beauty. I thought of how Frankie was able to make anybody do anything anytime, and how my path to that would be through my body. Now that I was sexually active, I understood better the effect I had on men. They wanted me.

But I had no interest in taking advantage of that, just a mild sense of importance and power that gave ballast to my overwhelming self-doubt. Being alone with a man—or with anybody, for that matter—made me recoil, desperately unable to communicate something like my true self. On the dance floor, I *was* myself—uninhibited, happy, loving.

Maybe dance countered church, which had consumed so much of my young life, but now waned as an influence. After a sort of hiatus, Mom switched to Pleasant Valley Church, where I would go in the morning, after an all-night binge of sweat and lust and pleasure. Pleasant Valley had been called The Old Cornerstone Church, which is how it was known when Grandma Kata headed its Sunday School and Bible Studies classes. I still believed wholeheartedly in God and salvation and all of that, but I became cynical about religion, or at least religion as we practiced it, such that on Sundays, getting ready for church, I'd think of the Monkees' "Pleasant Valley Sunday." The lyrics spoke to me. I keyed into the song's rebellion against boredom, misunderstanding its criticism of status and materialism. I didn't understand that I was becoming the kind of person the narrator wanted to escape.

We flitted from Alberini's to Town & Country, a place I'd known since I was a little girl. My friend Marie Dunning's mom worked there, and we would go for parties that included big-named stars in town, as part of the summer stock circuit. I'd met Barbara Eden, George Hamilton, and Ethel Merman, among others. I couldn't help but think that those people were more special than the ordinary people that populated my life. That was how everybody treated them. I guess, looking back, that my experiences with these stars, as well as Mom's desire to make me a beauty queen, helped prime me for my affair with Frankie. I unconsciously learned that to be adored was an achievable goal, and *not* to be adored was… not exactly a failure, but *ordinary*. If only *that* April had known that neither she nor anybody else was strictly ordinary, and that being the star of your own life was reward enough.

We buzzed out of Town & Country, over to The Living Room, then Cherry's Top of the Mall. At no time during my romps with Aunt Gigi and Big Chuck did I ever run into my classmates, because, of course, I was still years underage and so were all my peers. I was an adolescent living an adult life, though not completely, not always.

In other ways, at least to the naked eye, high school was going well. I was voted Best Dressed and Best Body, and the yearbook editors noted that my perfect career would be to open a modeling and charm school. What the editors did not know was that, for me, the charm circuit had run its course—it no longer inspired or motivated me. And yet, I continued to do the rounds, winning Miss Ohio and then placing fifth runner-up in Miss Teen USA in Tulsa, where Oral Roberts College lay like a wolf baring its teeth. I was exhausted with the pageants, vaguely unsettled about the hollow accolades, nervous and maybe a little bitter with the growing sense that all this effort would lead me nowhere. I wanted to be *somewhere*.

Twirling still filled my Friday nights, at least for the home football games. I got a jolt of adrenaline from performing in front of a raucous crowd, took satisfaction in going out to do something at which I was genuinely skilled. But these days, especially on cold, wet dark Ohio nights, with our little lives outlined by high-voltage stadium lights, I just wanted to be through with it.

And there were boys. Boys consumed our thoughts and our conversations. Boys made us smile or frown. Boys made or ruined our days. Boys toilet papered our houses, gave us lawn jobs, threw stuff in our pool. Now that I was intimate with Frankie, I started to realize just how many upperclassmen were already sexually active, just like how getting a bad back opens you to a hidden world of bad-back people. I chatted with my friends about *Love Story*, and all the ways in which our own romantic lives would resemble those portrayed in the film. Each time a large group of birds swarmed by, we would call out, "My wedding." The larger the group of birds, the larger the number of people that would attend our wedding. We did this strolling to the ice cream stand down at the end of our street, or walking to one of our houses, where we would play Monopoly or Parcheesi.

I'd started dating Bill Crain's brother, Dale Crain, who was 13 years my senior, and in so doing, further isolated myself from my own peers. I liked Dale and I wanted his attention. I wanted all the boys' attention, and I usually got it. But, in my mind, I was just occupying my time between meetings with Frankie. In later years, I would complain about the way men treated me—their infidelities, their insensitivity, their crass behavior—but in all my non-Frankie trysts during these formative years, it was I who treated my partners poorly. I used them for companionship, but refused to allow myself to commit. I was sweet, sometimes generous, but always, at the core, inaccessible.

And I did meet Frankie, in Heinz Hall in Pittsburgh, the Carrier Dome in Syracuse, The Cathedral in New Castle, Sharon High School Auditorium in Sharon. These days, you'd call these meetings hook-ups, but back then, I thought of them as something more romantic. I thought of them as an important part of my relationship with Frankie—they were meetings of love as much as of sex.

My relationship with Frankie was a family affair, and since my relatives sensed this was going to end badly for me, they increasingly got into tiffs with Frankie. Once, I convinced Kathy to drive with me to Pontiac, Michigan, where Frankie had booked us a room in the Hilton near his own. We did not tell our parents. "I have gas money!" I assured Kathy. "I have food money! Toll money! I've got it all mapped out!" We drove for four hours, laughing and plotting how to make this night one for the books.

Once there, Kathy settled into our room, and I went over to Frankie's. He opened the door, naked, his flaccid penis hung like a proud rearview mirror ornament. We kissed. He walked over and patted the bed. I undressed and crawled into bed. Just as foreplay commenced, and with that rearview mirror ornament pinging to attention, the phone rang. "It's for you," Frankie whispered. Warmth engulfed me as Kathy screamed, "We're going home!" Kathy's parents had found us out. I told Frankie I had to go, and he said, "Let me walk you downstairs," and "We'll get together again." He did not chastise me. He did not blame me, or even express disappointment. I remembered that. Kathy, the whole time, was hysterical, and when the pandemonium died down, I was sulking in the passenger seat on the long trip back. I thought, all the way, about how kind and gentle Frankie had been in the face of my embarrassment. His sweet eyes. His gentle good-bye. That he understood. Meanwhile, Aunt Lerene and Uncle Larry, furious, were waiting up at home.

Another time, I traveled to Pittsburgh with Uncle Chuck and Aunt Ginny. Pittsburgh in the mid-70s was known for its nightlife, and we were determined to make the rounds. Uncle Chuck assumed the identity of Gavatino Guitirus, and we played along. Uncle Chuck and Aunt Ginny effortlessly made friends with everybody at the bar, naturally made it a party, and with three hours to kill until show time, I broke from my usual ritual of just one alcoholic beverage. Instead, I had… many. Gigi and Chuck stole away to their room, and I went down to the bar and accepted a drink, then another, from friendly men. Returning, a bit wobbly, I threw up all over my silky jade jump suit. Then, with Aunt Ginny taking command, I was in the bathtub, naked. Eventually, Aunt Ginny had to dress me like one of my Barbie dolls, Uncle Chuck ironed my dress, and off we went to the concert hall.

These local nights out, like tonight, were my way of practicing to be without Frankie. We went from the Niles Strip to Austintown, and lost Kathy along the way to an early night. We danced again at Upstairs Lounge. With my high heels and blonde hair, I pushed an arm over my head, very slow, not too long. I noticed the men noticing me. I wondered what it would be like to just replace Frankie, to get another man who did for me what Frankie did, only did it all the time. Dale? Soon, Gigi and Big Chuck begged off. "No, don't go!" I pleaded. "Let's go to Perkins!" Perkins on Belmont Avenue and the nearby strip of hotel bars near my house were often the last stops. But go they did, and I supposed it was time for me to call it a night, as well.

As I watched Gigi and Big Chuck leave, I spotted Russell Sadie, who acknowledged me with a smile and waved me over. Russell's brother owned the Upstairs Lounge, and he was well known around town because he was a stunning human being. All the women loved to look at Russell, and lots of them did much more than that. Now, alone, with my one-drink buzz, I was in a desperate mood, desperate and lonely, desperate enough to confide in Russell my affair with Frankie.

"Frankie Valli?" Russell echoed. "I banged Mary Ann in Las Vegas."

Russell's reply seemed disjointed, a non sequitur, and he must have noted my confusion.

"His wife," Russell clarified. "Frankie Valli's *wife*, Mary Ann. I banged her. She was drunk and pissed off as hell at Frankie for something or another. We had fun."

*Wife?* The shock and epiphany came simultaneously, like when you discover the source of all your discomfort has been, all along, a rock in your shoe.

To Russell, it was nothing—swapping war stories. To me, it was a monumental setback. In a flash, I realized that my dream of marrying Frankie was just that, and that there was not a road to realization—there never had been. I did not want to be just another clerical kid mastering how to balance a checkbook. I wanted to call Frankie, to see Frankie, to scream at Frankie, to crawl in Frankie's arms. But of course, the best I could do was leave a message with his manager and wait until tomorrow or Monday, maybe mid-week, to hear back.

That should have been the moment when fragile, naïve, anxious April straightened her spine, wiped her high heels clean, and started to rearrange her future. But no. In the darkened Upstairs Lounge, with smoke and Frank Sinatra twirling in the air, half listening to Russell babble onward, I began to think,

*Their marriage is in trouble.*

*Frankie is unhappy with Mary Ann.*

*Mary Ann is unhappy with Frankie.*

*Frankie will soon be free.*

By the time I pulled down my hunter-green shades, rubbed my sore dancing feet under my Kelly green bedspread, and popped my birth control pill in my mouth, I had convinced myself that this revelation was all for the good. It put into focus the nature of our relationship, and gave plausible reasons why it had never escalated. Frankie was not free to commit. Soon, though… soon he would be, and then the April-Frankie love affair would be official, out in the open, and a glorious site for all to behold.

*April twirls the baton as the Liberty High School marching band performs at Liberty Leopards Stadium on Senior Night, 1975.*

# A STAND-IN FOR THE STAND-IN

I swayed and tapped and lip-synched the words to "Lady Marmalade," the cover band a ghostly apparition in the haze of the bar's cobalt blue lighting and thick smoke. Alberini's exquisite antiques shimmered in the distance. From across the bar came this model-beautiful man dressed in high-waist chocolate pants and matching polyester shirt. It was a Friday night and the football team was away; I was enjoying a rare night out in this, my senior year—*my* time, *my* place, *my* life.

I leaned against my wing girl, Kathy, sipping my Diet Coke and vodka as he drew near. Mom used to say, "Always carry a drink, but throw half of it in a plant so nobody takes advantage of you." I wore a soft Malachite jumpsuit, with a slight v-neck and a belt made out of the same silky polyester, with white high heels and a purse to match. Paris-green eye shadow drew out my hazel eyes, and emerald sparkles popped out of my style glasses.

Dozens of other sweaty men and women stood around—nobody ever sat—while dozens more danced. The men mostly wore pressed jeans and open-necked shirts; this guy had a distinct style in comparison. He had panache!

Alberini's was famous for its fabulous homemade food and, amongst the decadent crowd, a four a.m. liquor license. It was a stop on every carouser's agenda, but also a place where families enjoyed portions large enough to satisfy a brown bear. It was the kind of place you could take home Italian pastries, fresh warm bread, or your wedding soup; and also the kind of place where you could see big guys in fancy sweat suits roughly escorting somebody to the parking lot.

He walked up to me with his drink in his hand and said, "Take off your glasses." I obliged. "I want to see your face when I tell you I'm going to marry you," he said.

Phillip was not a star, but he could have played one on TV. He doubled for Tom Selleck in *Magnum P.I.*, gorgeous all the way, from his tan, highlighted hair to the cigarette dangling from his manicured hand. We danced and we talked, talked and danced, and at one point the inevitable question arose, "What music do you listen to?"

As always in these social situations, I froze, unable to retrieve honest and intelligent thoughts. I said, "Oh, I don't know much about music. But I am a big Frankie Valli fan and mostly listen to him."

Was that what I really was, his *fan*? Maybe so.

We small talked some more, in that way that, under the spell of attraction, made the trivial seem monumental. I told Phillip about my upcoming job interview at a local clothing store, Rappold's, at the Eastwood Mall. He shared this and that, but really focused on me. He listened to my stories and interjected only to ask pertinent questions that showed genuine interest. He laughed at my jokes. He urged me to reveal more about myself. That he was charmed, I found charming. Thus, the courtship began, and make no mistake: this *was* a courtship. Unlike Frankie, with whom it was sex and hotel bars and concert halls, Phillip wooed me. He wooed hard.

In the morning, I found myself opening a special delivery: twenty albums all wrapped up with a bow on top. Bread, Chicago, Seals and Croft, The Temptations, Commodores, Luther Vandross, Barry White, and more. Also: a beautiful khaki suit and a matching pale top with a neatly handwritten note saying, "Good luck with your job interview, and now you have plenty of great music."

I thought back on the previous evening, trying to recall if, in my giddiness and half-buzzed state, I hinted at my relationship with Frankie. If so, was this Phillip's way of getting me to move on from Frankie and onto him?

I was a Golden Leopard Liberty High School senior, soon to be a co-ed, living on yogurt, Cheerios, and bags of crackers, swiping toilet paper from the Union restroom. Phillip, on the other hand, flashed importance, spent money like there was no end in sight to it. He pampered me, treated me like a queen, said and did all the things that made me believe I was not his hobby but his vocation.

We ate fancy dinners at The Tangiers in Akron, the shoreline cafes in Cleveland, the La Mont in Pittsburgh. In Washington, D.C. we rode a lift up to Ollie's Trolley restaurant, the price of the stunning panoramic views included with the flavored butters and juicy steaks. At The Playboy Club in Chicago, I watched a bunny fluff her tail in Phillip's face as she left our table.

I suppose I thought this was a contrast to Frankie, and I suppose I was old enough to know better. I should have looked at the similarities. Phillip was—*again*—an older man, 12 years my senior. Phillip was—*again*—married. Phillip was—*again*—mired in his own problems.

So during my senior year, I shuffled off to faraway places under Phillip's tutelage. If Frankie taught me sex, Phillip endeavored to teach me sophistication. He tutored me on how to dress, how to act, what to eat, what to do and not to do. I accepted his wisdom. I let myself be his clay. Meanwhile, I did not go to Prom, nor did I join the fun on Skip Day, nor even the State Fair. I did not participate in any school activities because I did everything with Phillip, and Phillip was a man, not a student.

I first discovered that Phillip was married three months into things. Les, for all his faults, was not only protective, but had good intuition. He knew there was something funny about Phillip. He pulled some strings with his former state cop buddies, who ran the license plate on Phillip's fully loaded gold Lincoln town car with white leather interior. Soon, Les was triumphantly reporting back the results, and I was rushing off to confront Phillip with an ultimatum. "If you ever get divorced, give me a call." I did this in dramatic fashion—agreeing to a driving trip and waiting until the moment at which we were about to cross Pittsburgh's scenic 6th Street Bridge to blurt my accusations.

But I failed to understand that liberation would only happen for me when A) I established priorities, and B) I made choices that adhered to my own values, hard as they might seem. It was about character. Who was I? Who did I want to be? As long as I allowed men to dictate my value, I could never find confidence, much less satisfaction. Here, on that bridge, I thought I was dictating the terms, but really I was only demanding a concession. I did not then, nor for a long time after, appreciate that intelligence and kindness were more important than mushroom champagne risotto or really great breasts, that security was not an old man bankrolling my life but rather confidence in my own capabilities. This is not to dismiss fine things or beauty, just to relegate them to their proper place in the scheme of things. I never gave myself credit for my qualities that lurked beneath the surface, so convinced was I that I was a minor leaguer who had been somehow gifted a major league roster spot.

During my whirlwind romance with Phillip, I never stopped

thinking about Frankie. I would pose with a delicate forkful of almond-crusted salmon and wish Frankie were there to see it. I would kick up sand on South Beach and wonder what Frankie would think of me now. I would recline in my first-class seat en route to Italy and wonder whether Frankie would be impressed. At the same time, I convinced myself that the past was the past and that I was perfectly content with my *now*. But with Phillip seemingly out of the picture, I reverted to full stalking mode, hunting down Frankie in Toledo and sleeping with him again—for pleasure, revenge, maybe even renewal of hope. I had sort of convinced myself that I'd return to Frankie a wizened woman, a woman who'd been out in the world, a woman who had plenty of other opportunities and was merely choosing one. I thought Frankie would see that I was in high demand—I thought, I don't know, that he would read this on my face or the way I moved my hips—and that he'd do well to pin me down. But as always with Frankie, a romp was just a romp was just a romp.

In no time at all, Phillip returned, delivering the news that he was leaving his wife. Divorce proceedings were under way. I knew little about his relationship then. Only later did I hear news of an awful and tense marriage that Phillip had been desperate to escape. I was his getaway driver. Maybe he loved me—I think he truly did—but if I'm being honest, I never loved him. Rather, it seemed as though I was carried along into marriage through some hurricane force whose intensity exceeded all possible warnings.

And I was warned. Ginny, Les, Mom, Grandma Kata—their condemnation of the relationship was universal. One day, Aunt Lerene, Mom's blood sister, came upon me ironing Phillip's shirts. She said, "April, what are you doing? You're 18 years old, ironing some man's clothes. This man is going to get old on you fast." But here I was, almost not a teenager anymore, all grown up, or so I thought, wanting to start a life out of earshot of the banging and screaming, wanting a true and equal seat at the table with my aunt, begging, I suppose, to start my life.

Senior Band Night I sobbed on the playing field where I'd poured so much sweat into becoming a star. I don't know whether I cried because it was over, or because I missed it while it was happening. I looked at my glittery costume and my maroon and gold corsage with a gold bell, and thought, "What now?" I was scared. Lonely. Indecisive. More importantly, I did not understand that what I was feeling was perfectly natural and common, and that introspection was healthy. Instead, I thought some immediate action was required. Les and Mom were there to hug and "there, there" me, but I guess part of my fear was knowing that they had long since been eliminated as fixed points on the horizon.

Phillip, meanwhile, spoiled me rotten. He gave me a Louis Vuitton bag, whisked me off to West Palm Beach for a round of golf at Doral Country Club, and off again for a game of jai alai near Dania Beach.

I lasted about one minute at Oral Roberts University. Everywhere I walked, I ran into The Man himself: a huge mural of him, buildings named after him or his family, monuments to his greatness. Right from the beginning, I did not want to be in that creepy place named after that creepy man, and so I quickly transferred to Bowling Green State University. I majored in television/radio production until I almost cut my finger off in a splicing machine. By the time the blood dried, I had started to figure out how to transfer to Youngstown State University, and what classes I needed to take to be a counselor. Having spent a lot of time around dysfunction, I figured being a counselor would be a chance to help others, and maybe also myself in the process.

That freshman year in college, I tried, minimally, to do what college kids did. I attended fraternity parties, zonked out in my sweatpants after an all-night cram session, people watched at Kilcawley Center. But I had little time for typical college stuff, because I was going back and forth between Youngstown and

Toledo to see Phillip, or Phillip was coming to Toledo to see me. We were absolutely busy with extravagant whatnot.

On trips home, Mom's deterioration was ever more apparent, as though she'd stopped trying. She had a private phone installed in Grandma Kata's basement, where she stayed whenever she wasn't working or gallivanting. She made her intention clear: she wanted out of her marriage. Jeffrey and Les were batching it back at the house. With me gone, Jeffrey was now the spoiled one: he had go-carts, a mini motorcycle, and a horse stabled up the street.

Unlike Mom, I hadn't stopped trying. But I deferred my own interests to Phillip's, even turning down a dancing audition at Fordham University in New York City. Phillip didn't want me to go, and I can't even remember why. I just said, "Okay," and looked at the Midwest sky, blue like a robin's egg. "What color is the sky in New York City?" I wondered.

The only breaks from Phillip were Frankie breaks. I would orchestrate a temporary breakup in order to accept a Frankie invitation to a concert here or there. At the time, I thought I was sticking to some sort of moral code, that I was being monogamous, but really I was just creating the conditions under which I could get off on a technicality.

Why did I continue to pursue my relationship with Frankie? It's complicated, of course. Facing the truth is hard for a young woman, and I was no exception. Frankie was my addiction, and I did not want to kick the habit. I suppose I saw hope in Frankie, and I was desperate to keep that hope alive. Evidence that this was a ruined relationship was all around, out in the open to be gathered by any industrious forensic scientist of the heart. I saw those clues, but I didn't want to believe them. And so, when I reunited with Frankie, as I did in Pittsburgh, Cleveland, and Syracuse, I chose to accept simple lies and avoidances, knowing that the alternative was a tense tryst, suspecting that the outcome would be a bullet to our romance rather than a successful surgery.

These reunions were more of the same—screwing, singing, rubbing elbows, making vague promises to do this again. Don't get me wrong: I loved the screwing. I loved the singing. I loved the rubbing elbows. But the whole experience always left me hollow and insecure, a tad stricken that *this* was life—in and out, in and out, in and out—and before the blush had left my face, I was back with Phillip, being grand.

*Why* is the companion to every *what*. Detectives cannot solve a murder without a motive—that and a dead body. Over and over again, I chose to keep Frankie on life support, and without the body, I couldn't begin to solve the crime. With Phillip, I thought I could finally let Frankie die, and in so doing, work the case.

*Okay* is also what I said to Phillip's marriage proposal. The whole marriage could be summed up in a tweet—140 characters seem about right to summarize our single year of matrimony. In Phillip's never-ending quest to impress me, and my own never-ending penchant for being impressed, he proposed via a champagne-bearing parachuter who landed near our outdoor patio table at Toledo's glittery On the Green. A three-and-a-half carat diamond ring followed, and then a classy rehearsal at Albirini's, where we'd first met. Everyone was there, even the restaurant's owners.

The marriage was not going to last, regardless of everything else—and the *everything else* was considerable. Phillip was a stand-in for Frankie, who perhaps was a stand-in for my father. I, of course, didn't know I was missing the point. My happiness could never be granted to me; I would need to earn it on my own. Only then, when I was content with myself, might a man add to my happiness, round out my life. But I wasn't there, not yet. I could move on from Frankie in body, but not in mind.

I plowed forward to my wedding day despite deep misgivings—I still felt something for Frankie and was not sure I felt the same about Phillip. When the day came, I fixed and fussed in my childhood bedroom. I was 19 years old. My antique white wedding dress stood as a false symbol, and the long, long lace train dragged further behind me than all of my years on Earth. I was alone. It was quiet. I stared at my face in the mirror, a beautiful face, I'd been told time and time again, but a face wrought with worry. From downstairs in the kitchen, I heard the phone ring, and then strained to catch Les huffing his end of the conversation. I could not make out much, but it sounded serious. I snapped my garter. I strained some more, as Mom and Les huddled in their own bedroom, raising their whispers to nearly audible levels.

Next, Mom entered my room, gingerly, with a World's-About-To-End look on her face. "April Lynn," she said. "We need to have a discussion."

Mom summarized the phone conversation Les had just concluded. Some man, identity unknown, had called to caution me against marrying Phillip. The man said he knew of me and wouldn't feel right letting the marriage happen without my knowing that Phillip was a degenerate gambler on a road to Nothing Good. "She don't want to get involved with this guy," is the way the anonymous caller had put it.

"If you want to back out of this," Mom started, "you can."

Dazed, confused, I stared at my garter.

"Nobody will feel bad," Mom added.

I've never examined the ways that my female role models influenced my behavior towards men. As a teenager, then as a young adult, even now, I've always thought: I'm my own woman. I make my own decisions. The mistakes and triumphs are my own. At the core, I believe that is true. But during those tender early years, what I saw—the older men, the married men, the perverts, the sexual abusers—became a part of a landscape that seemed normal. I was too young to question whether it was healthy. I didn't know clinical terms like *co-dependence* or *statutory rape* or *infidelity*. I just knew that Mom and many other women in my family did these things, and nobody caught on fire.

In so many ways, Mom, Aunt Ginny, and Grandma Kata were trying to raise me to be a different kind of strong female. Because, make no mistake: for all their flaws, my female relatives were incredible. In so many ways. Their accomplishments, big and small, could fill a whole other book. They loved me. They cared for me. They pampered me. They encouraged me to get an education, to strive to become my best self. I saw all that. But I also saw their men, hitting and slamming, carousing, sneaking, lying, two-timing, three-timing, four-timing. Not that the men were all bad, not nearly. Bumpy and even Les continued, over the years, to try to make our lives good: working hard, protecting us, and rallying their efforts for family celebrations or crises. These men were the product of a society and generation that did not fully respect women, and these women, I suppose, did not fully believe they could command such respect.

Suddenly Mom—Mom, who'd married incredibly young, who'd divorced, who'd always chosen older men, who'd stayed in an abusive relationship, who'd cheated, who'd lied—suddenly, Mom was telling me, "Don't do this! Don't marry so young! This man is too old for you! This man will hurt you!"

But I would not listen.

I was becoming like my women role models, only I didn't know it. Objectively, Frankie Valli was *the wrong guy*. He was 24 years older than me. I mean, My God! At a time when I should have been learning about love with boys my own age, I was the total subject of a middle-aged man. I was the concubine kissing the feet of the Emperor. The way Frankie viewed our relationship could not match my own view, and a smarter woman would have said, "Thanks, no." Smart and 19 don't always go together, though.

Phillip, too, was *the wrong guy*. Old enough to be my teacher. Married and out prowling when I met him. A compulsive gambler, apparently. This, again, should have been an easy "Thanks, but no thanks" situation, and here I had an out—a relatively face-saving reason to do what was right for me and call off the wedding. But I did not want to hurt Phillip's feelings; I wanted to move out of my parents' house and into the apartment Phillip and I had already rented and furnished and decorated; I wanted to continue being half of the foursome with Uncle Chuck and Aunt Ginny; I wanted the fine meals and exotic trips to continue.

Mom left me alone to think it over. I wish that I'd understood the value of being alone, of knowing *how to* be alone. Simply put, I never in my life allowed any cracks between relationships, always going from one to another to another, possibly to avoid ever having to face myself.

I spent hours alone in my room, thinking. I thought, "Why did this caller wait until now?"

"How do we even know it was true?"

"Maybe it was partly true, but not nearly as bad as all that."

"How sad would Phillip be if I didn't go through with this?"

Until that point, I had not known that Phillip gambled. I knew that he was overly interested in sports, especially college football, and that he got stressed beyond imagination watching the games. But I hadn't questioned that; I hadn't even questioned where he got so much money, except for the fact that he had a decent job and a rich family—his dad had created jai alai in Florida, and his aunt invented Pond's cold cream.

We went through with the charade: wedding pictures at home, limo rides, the beautiful church ceremony, the lavish reception, cookies from just about every Youngstown kitchen occupying more space than was reserved for the dance floor. Well wishes and gifts. Crying, hugging, kissing. Before the evening ended, my ridiculously long train had been shredded, surely a symbol of what was to come.

It wasn't until we were on our honeymoon in Aruba that I confronted Phillip about his supposed gambling problem. We fought. We didn't speak for three days. Blonde beaches and gently lapping surf and swaying divi-divi trees provided background to our tense, already-broken relationship. By the time we returned home to our new married-life abode, this much was clear: Phillip was broke. He returned to his drafting job with the Mahoning County Engineers and continued to borrow family money to squeak past the most hazardous spots. I continued my undergraduate education. Nine months into it, we were seated at a dark booth at the Great Gatsby in Austintown when two gorillas in suits, gold jewelry, and big rings approached our table. "We need to speak privately for a minute, Mr. Regano."

The place was crowded. I looked from one table to another, expecting somebody, everybody, to see the panic in my eyes, to understand the emergency in which we all found ourselves. But it was not their emergency. Back then, Youngstown was known as Mob Town, USA. I feared that a Godfather held our fate. I popped up from the table, raced to the payphone in the lobby, and called Uncle Chuck. He said he'd see what could be done. The clock was ticking. The music continued, people danced, people ate, people chitchatted. Twenty minutes passed. Phillip emerged from the back room rumpled and out of sorts, scared, belittled, hurt, though not so much physically.

By now, things were bad. *Bad* bad. We ran up our credit card debt to fund a simple life. Phillip came home beaten, sometimes physically, sometimes spiritually. He refused to seek help. What he did instead was go out and buy a water pistol that looked remarkably like a real .45 caliber pistol. He planned to bluff his way out of the next predicament.

Meanwhile, I'd won a small part in a Youngstown University production of *Kismet*, in which I was made to dance at the feet of the beautiful Billy Kirkwood, a rebel musician and half-hearted undergraduate, enormously talented and passionate and charming. By the time I rose and looked him in the eye, Phillip was as good as gone.

*April and Phillip attend high school graduation party at Aunt Ginny's house, 1975.*

# BILLY BALL

The word "kismet" means "fate" or "destiny." Turned into a musical, *Kismet* becomes a twisty tale of love, lust, luck, and plain lasciviousness, and it involves poets, beggars, thieves, and so much more. The Youngstown State University theatre department meant to do this story justice, while I, at least initially, meant to do away with the gym credit I needed to eventually finish my degree work at YSU, to where I'd transferred.

But I, and Billy Kirkwood, got caught up in the web of intrigue.

Billy played the Prince, whose family endeavors to find him a suitable wife. I played a belly dancer striving to be the princess, but who ultimately gets rejected. I wore shimmery, layered sheer scarves in shades of peach and rose, matching balloon pants rolled down my hips, and a sequined top. The outfit was one part Jeannie and one part Charo. The director cautioned me to "pull back," since my role was to be unsuitable, not desirable, but I couldn't help myself, and even, on opening night, took a bow with the play's stars, only to be chastised for not knowing my place as a bit player.

I knew from the first that I wanted Billy, and found my heart full of deceit even before I'd done Phillip any wrong. While Phillip was out, I posed in front of our bedroom's double full-length mirror with the "Presentation of Princesses" playing on our boom box. I writhed and twirled and bucked to the rollicking eastern chimes, stopping to wipe the sweat from my cheek. I stared at the bead of sweat slowly dripping down from my belly button, and wriggled my pants lower. I wet my index finger and raised a line from the top of my pubic region to above my waistband, hoping to darken the line of hair pointing south.

Our paths hardly crossed anymore. Phillip worked or golfed, and I was busy with school, studying and going to class. The gambling problems came down on our head immediately and ruined both our literal and figurative honeymoons. We started with the tension and fatigue and fear that usually doom couples much later. We skipped the part where we were thrilled to be together, unified against the world.

I was the line captain of the YSU band, and also on the dance line, so just as I had been in my teenaged life before, I was busy and ambitious. The difference was that now, I was married.

Billy Kirkwood was six-foot-four, trim, with a broad smile, blue eyes, and a thick mane of curly hair. He was at YSU on a music scholarship, playing first chair trumpet in the school band and moonlighting on the club circuit, first in a popular polka band, which he eventually gave up in favor of a rock band, and then a cover band, and finally a large funk band.

We fell into the habit of playing pool at the Kilcawley Center after rehearsals, and the flirting escalated with each game of Last Pocket. By opening night, my scene in which I danced at the Prince's feet had turned very real to me, and I wanted the Prince to choose me. The college production lasted just one weekend and then we disbanded, though not Billy and I. He invited me to see one of his shows, and then a rehearsal.

Watching Billy lovingly work those trumpet keys with his fingers, sensually blow that horn with his luscious lips, was, for me, an erotic experience. Staring at the thin layer of sweat bead on his upper lip, watching his intense concentration, seeing his hips swivel and sway, reminded me of those early days of my awakening, the moisture and ache so intense that I wanted, right there, to slide my hands down my pants and make myself come.

Here I was, déjà vu, back to the early days with Frankie, crooning over a crooner, falling in love with the music and the man, the man and the music. Billy was talented, too. But in many ways, Billy was the antithesis of Frankie—and of Phillip, too, for that matter.

He grew up in a strict Pentecostal family, like my own, and first-chaired the National Youth Choir. His was a small family living outside New Castle, Pennsylvania, in a town called Bessemer. Everything about his background—from the backyard's kiddy pool and broken wooden swing, to his street's identical row houses, to the aluminum siding—seemed to declare that this was a simple, struggling life.

Like me, Billy grew up fast. He started playing in a polka band at age 15, where he first got a taste for nightlife and women, including, apparently, Liza Minnelli in New York City. He'd had Liza; I'd had Frankie—call it a draw.

When I met him, he wore his poor artist stature on his sleeve, driving around a beat-up red Chevy, bumming cigarettes, and wearing scuffed and cobbled shoes. But despite all that, or maybe because of it, Billy sizzled with sexuality. His signature white t-shirt and faded Levi's, along with his ever-present cigarette, invited heated stares. He even skipped meals, as though fornicating were all the nourishment he needed. He drove fast, so fast that he accumulated a prodigious number of speeding tickets on his trips to and from Bessemer, a routine that inspired the Poland Township Police to call his home and advise he take another route from that point forward.

Billy was 18; I was 20. This was 1978, the summer *Grease* exploded onto the pop culture scene. Frankie Valli was everywhere, with the title track from the movie getting airtime every second of every day. A whole new generation of fans were discovering Frankie for the first time, and I felt jealous, bitter, happy, and despondent all at once. I'd hear "Grease" and picture Frankie singing to me. I'd imagine him staring into the eyes of some young girl who was in essence the new me; Frankie making love to his wife; Frankie thrilling his adoring fans. I'd mostly given up on having Frankie to myself, on having Frankie forever, but his omnipresence foiled my plan to forget about him. Phillip hadn't helped me forget. Anxiety seemed to cause me to revert back to those old dreams, and when Phillip came home beaten over gambling debts, or when he schemed on the phone to raise quick cash, or when he instructed me that we'd have to postpone paying utilities, I became *very* anxious—for his welfare, for my welfare, for our futures.

One day, I cut my American Poets class to go, alone, to the Eastwood Mall and see *Grease.* By then, I had stopped talking at all about Frankie, in part out of deference to my new husband, in part out of embarrassment for my lingering hopeless fantasies. It was my first time going to a movie theatre alone. As the coming attractions played, I sipped a gigantic drum of Diet Coke. I was not going to go to Hollywood. I was not going to go to New York. Here I was, married, a college student, somebody with a present and a future. I thought about my class load: Special Education 101, Children's Literature, American Poets, Economics, Accounting 101. Soon, I would have my bachelors, and from there, I would work toward my certification in English education. In light of these plans, my Frankie fantasies were humiliating.

I secretly checked out each new moviegoer who entered the theater and found their seats. I was sure that I would know somebody—or, more to the point, that they would know me. I was also sure, as soon as I was recognized, that the whole game would be up: April Gatta was here, by herself, goggling over her ex-lover and pretending, praying, plotting that the whole affair would start again. I even rehearsed my response: I, April, was stressed from study and needed a mental health day, and, oh, sure, I'd been involved with Frankie but wished him luck and thought it would be fun to see his latest triumph, as an old friend and well-wisher.

The more I contemplated my life—Phillip, my studies, my home—the more I realized I was not passionate about anything. I did not have a passion. The movie started, and there, bigger than life, was Frankie. I had mixed emotions. I reminded myself that I wasn't completely nuts, that Frankie had wanted me, had *had* me, that it was not just a case of some doe-eyed fan bagging a star. It had been, at least on the margins, a romance. I continued to think, "Only if…" Only if I were classier. Only if I were smarter. Only if I were more amazing in bed. For the longest time, Frankie had been my passion, but now? Was all my work, all my choices, making me into a woman worthy of Frankie Valli?

Frankie appeared again at the end of the movie, and soon I transitioned from darkness to light. Staring up at that big orange ball in the sky, I felt the dread of seeing before me the postscript to what was once *everything* to me.

But then there was Billy. Here was this young stud, a sex symbol not unlike John Travolta's Danny, who shook and thrusted to Frankie's vocals. Here was this musician playing the pants off young hotties, just like Frankie. Here was this man, charming and seductive and a bit dangerous, just like Frankie. I was not nearly far enough along in my psychological studies to understand the term "imprinting," but had I been, I might have recognized what was happening here, as I found yet another substitute for a prototype I'd followed blindly since just after kindergarten.

One night, some months into our friendship, I watched

Billy's band rehearse on Market Street. Afterward, Billy and I danced over and over to Michael Jackson's "Rock with You." We were giggly. We were sweaty. We were aroused. Billy offered me a ride home, an offer that both of us knew meant something more. On the car ride home, Billy glanced at me from behind the wheel and said, "Look at you: you're absolutely stunning."

I wore hip-hugger blue jeans and a snow-white sleeveless tee, a little white cotton bra, and white cotton panties, along with white cowboy boots. Call it my White Phase. Neither of us mentioned Phillip, but we were both thinking about him. He was waiting at home, presumably, and when Billy's car pulled up to our apartment, that would be that. "Thanks for the ride," I would say, and then the moment would be gone, maybe forever. Reflection is the enemy of rash behavior.

"Turn here," I urged, and Billy obeyed. He did not ask any questions as I directed him away from my address, as though he had vast experience in the ways and means of the discreet, dirty, forbidden affair. "Right there," I said. "Turn off your lights."

We were at the end of Millicent Avenue, at the top of the old gravel hill, nothing but trees, the spot to which I used to walk every day to catch the school bus, somewhere between Mom's house and Grandma's house, a long, winding, unpaved side street, dark but for the faint glow of street lamps here and there. "They're home, but they'll never even know we're here," I declared.

Our first kiss was everything I had fantasized about. My ache crescendoed. Desire started to feel like need. Billy was behind the wheel, I in the passenger seat, the parking gear between us. He reclined his seat. There, in Billy's cramped Chevy, he fondled my nipples under my shirt, and I reached down to relieve his ache, and then, in the indirect lighting of a Youngstown growing more and more urban but clinging to its rural roots, I bowed my head, unzipped his faded jeans, and began slowly to work magic, lovingly brushing my lips against his skin, while he teased me with his nicotine-stained fingers, played me like a riveting trumpet solo. I was about to burst. I raised my head, tugged my jeans and lacy panties down to my ankles and then over my white cowboy boots, and swung my leg over the parking gear. I raised my charm school booty in the air long enough for Billy to yank his jeans and underwear down to his own ankles, and then I straddled him. I plunged down on him, he thrust into me, and we both came almost instantly.

All at once, I felt this enormous love, fear, regret, even panic. Suddenly those dim street lights seemed powerfully bright, and as I hugged Billy around the neck, both of us panting, I trained my eyes on Grandma Kata's front door, wondering who was there, what they were doing, and how much they might have seen. I could almost see my childhood through the darkness. Billy drove me home and dropped me off a few doors down, our relationship now, officially, relegated to the shadows. I lurked into the house and already knew that I couldn't do this. I was not wired to cheat.

While I'd stopped most all of my church activities, I could never change the foundation that those beliefs had pounded into me all through my childhood. I still considered a lie to another a lie to God, and within a short time, I was sitting down with Phillip telling him everything, including that I felt I was in love with Billy. I wanted Phillip to be over, and to share Billy with the rest of my world, which I could not do in secret.

But truth is sometimes a hard and reckless choice, and in short order, Phillip zoomed his gold aircraft carrier of a Lincoln over to Billy's little shack of a house, sat down in his tailored and pressed trousers on the Kirkwoods' shabby-but-clean couch, and shook his hand in the air with such rage that the crosses and Jesus pictures and plastic angels shook, too. The truth was, Phillip, at that moment, was as broke as the Kirkwoods, but ne'er-do-wells like Phillip tend to fall in silk parachutes onto well-manicured lawns.

Before smoke from the scene had settled, Phillip had

wrecked his car, Billy had been disowned by his deacon First Christian Assembly parents, and Mom, who'd opened the door to an unexpected knock, was worrying over what to do with this homeless lover of her married daughter.

*April, Love Bug, and Billy leaning on April's Triumph.*

# COLD TURKEY

So then, Billy and I were together. My marriage ended up, like Phillip's car, a big pile of metal, glass, and plastic shrapnel. Soon, I moved my old pink-and-white canopy bed back to my old bedroom in Mom's house. There wasn't really anything to split up. We didn't even have a joint checking account, because we'd funded everything on credit. I left Phillip the apartment, the furniture, and everything else, and in no time at all, he was hooked up with a girl from work.

Billy was waiting, and I loved him, I suppose, like a stray dog, which was sort of what he was. I still had Lovie, and now I had Billy.

I know now—God, I wish I knew then—that this was a formula for disaster. I was an emotional cripple, incapable of making the hard choices, uttering the hard no's. I went from one to the other "yes," thinking, all the time, that I had finally arrived, only to learn I was just changing planes again.

And the reason it was a disaster was because I disallowed myself time to think. Time to feel. Time to heal. I was allowing life to choose me, not the other way around.

Mom found Billy a house, just as she'd found Phillip and me an apartment. Mom rallied in an emergency; she thrived on chaos. It was like plugging in a toaster and watching the heater coils go red hot. If I were wounded, she'd patch me up; if I were healthy, she'd make me bleed (I suppose, just so she could patch me up again). This house wasn't down the block, but it was right behind us, one street over. It was the house Mom had inherited from her church friends, Sally and Stan Hertzog, a dying token of their appreciation for her volunteer help as their caregivers. Mom had done nothing with it since taking it over. It wasn't much anyway, but without care, it had grown dank and moldy. The utilities had long been turned off. We got Billy a mattress where he could sleep and we could make love, and for the rest of it, we could sort of make due.

Phillip and I had a lot of loose ends to tie up. He called to implore me to "Look at this guy's house! Look at his family!" He meant to tell me that I was trading down. We discussed formalized divorce proceedings. We powwowed about possessions. It was more polite than passionate, and as we moved from one thing to another, I tried with little luck to trace the cause of this obvious mistake.

Billy was, in a lot of ways, another mistake—already in the making, not even waiting. But we were in love, and so ever delighted to explore each other—anywhere, anytime—that we didn't consider the future. Except to say that my honesty, my insistence on bringing everything into the open, had left Billy with no safety net except me, and now, at 20, I felt the burden of having a failed marriage and an 18-year-old dependent.

But: love. We thought we had it, and I think we did, at least on some level. Indeed, it turned out to be a love that flickered and flamed and smoked and wavered for the next two decades, through a lot of good and bad times, through the birth of two incredible children, through cheating and scrimping and laughing, until it finally got snuffed out.

Billy essentially flunked out of YSU. He never could read music, and fell behind his more scholarly peers. He was never a great match with the prestigious Dana School of Music. Now, he had no family, no school, no steady job. Billy lived for performance, and his energy increased and his mood improved as the clock hands snuck past midnight, into the smoky, forbidden early hours of the morning. His new funk band, in which he was the only white musician in a large group filled with horns and percussion and strings, thrilled small crowds in bars all around the area. The energy in those tiny makeshift concert venues, on those tiny makeshift dance floors, was addictive. The whole room, as one, would sway and sweat, thump and tap, bob and bump. The band members—ten of them, at least—all wore white silk jumpsuits and capes, which they waved in the air as they sang songs like "Chameleon," "She's a Bad Mama Jama," "Cut The Cake," "Sex Machine," "Rock Steady," and more. Billy habitually drank, and he smoked a little weed, but never to great excess. It was almost just part of the job—some people punched a time clock, Billy grabbed his first light beer. He was happy and alive, and this was to be our weekends for a long time to come.

Soon, Billy and I took our own space, the upstairs of Mr. and Mrs. Barr's house in Hubbard, Ohio. Mr. and Mrs. Barr lived downstairs. The place was cheap, and I paid for everything, partly by selling my blue Triumph. The plan was that we'd both get full-time work, and Billy would supplement that income with his gig money. When Billy got paid, it was decent money, and Natural Force Band had started to make a reputation for itself, which meant more bookings.

Moving in together was rash, but it didn't feel like we had many options. Billy could not stay indefinitely in the Hertzog's crusty old house, and I could not continue to live at home. Now that I was essentially a full-grown woman, about to graduate from college, I understood Les a bit better, and not in his favor. I realized that the bitterness and anger I felt toward him were not always his fault, that as a little girl, I rejected a substitute father— it did not much matter whether it was Les or some higher-standard Les. But I also saw that Mom and Grandma Kata and Aunt Ginny were right in forbidding Les to be alone with me— he was surely a pervert and perhaps a tad mentally unsound. At one point, Phillip, who'd taken to showing up at the house weepy with regret and wild with hope, agreed to meet Les at the Liberty Donut Shop. Les had hinted there was big news, the kind of news that could only be shared face-to-face. Once there, Les opened a *Playboy* centerfold on the donut shop counter, declared to Phillip, "Look! April posed for *Playboy*. We have to do something! She's out of control!" Of course, the centerfold was not me, didn't much even look like me, but among other things, I started to see that Les thought of me not as a daughter but as a sex object.

I started working as an eligibility manager at Equitable Assurance on Market Street in Boardman, Ohio, where I processed all the paperwork for steel mills in Youngstown. Billy went to work at the Ohio State Department of Unemployment, processing claims. We had just one car, Billy's red Nova, the one with failing brakes and a rusty undercarriage, the one in which we'd first made love.

It was almost four years since my last encounter with Frankie. Like with AA members, I should have gotten a bronze recovery medallion; I was, no doubt, an addict. During times of stress, depression, or boredom, alcoholics turned to booze, addicts to drugs, and I to Frankie. During those clean years, I told myself I was done with Frankie; chided myself for the stupidity of the affair; hated him for not wanting me enough; hated myself for not making myself wanted; turned off his music mid-note.

I continued to think about him. In times of loneliness, like when I was holed up at home with a textbook while Billy played trumpet to drunk, horny fans, I would let my mind wander. When money got tight, as it always did, I fantasized, again, about the life of a rock star's wife. A fit of sadness over some slight at school, work, or home made me remember not the chill of being sent away but the warmth of being in Frankie's arms. It wasn't sexual, or at least not entirely so. It was about life: the one I had, versus the one I thought I wanted. It was about adventure. It was about self-esteem. It was about hope, the hope that I, April Gatta, the little country girl from the little rural town, would face the world as Somebody Special.

My life with Billy was fine, and I cherished his kindness, even though I already suspected he was, and would continue to be, way too generous with strange women. There was the rainstorm when Billy lifted me in his arms and carried me over the puddles to my office door, just so I wouldn't ruin my high heels. There were the fuzzy little ducks Billy brought home in his pockets, sure evidence that he understood my nature and was intent on making me happy. Then there was the time Billy jumped off the stage to do battle with a burley, Harley-riding chick who pushed me—an escapade that ended with the whole band being escorted from the bar. Billy never scolded me, blamed me, or made me feel guilty. He did not complain about burnt toast, tough pork chops, or my mother's enraging need to control. There was his smile, the great (and incredibly frequent) sex, the sense that we were in this together.

We lived for the weekends, out in the bars, dancing to the funk, drinking, staying out late, feeling the closeness and love of people united by music. I continued to be naïve, or at least overly trusting, but little tics of doubt registered in my mind. Billy smiling at a fan in a too-intimate way; groupies (yes, even little local bands got their share) dancing provocatively in front of the stage; random hot women flirting openly, thinking nothing of my presence. And that was just when I was there. Already, Billy would come home smelling of cigarettes and perfume, but he always assured me that was just the accumulated scent of seven hours in a tightly-packed bar.

Once I got my undergraduate degree, I continued on part-time at YSU, already at work on my second degree. It was an individualized program that included psychological communications, business, and English. I also started taking classes in mental health counseling, and geared up to apply for the full-time graduate program. It wasn't just that I was covering all my bases, but that I was pursuing strands of interest. Billy always supported this, but he was not intellectually curious in the same way. He only ever examined life closely through music.

We were close to home, or at least my home, but that was a mixed blessing. Mom was tired and wrinkled. She hopped from lover to lover, left and reunited with Les, and nearly died undergoing a complete face-lift. She had found her would-be surgeon on *Oprah*, tracked him to his practice in Cleveland, and signed up to slice and dice her way back to her youth, not anticipating that her unique blood type would put her in such peril when the operation went south. She recovered at Grandma Kata's, and also holed up there at other times, accepting suitors she attracted at work, in psychological treatment, even on her Mary Kay route, the one that almost earned her a pink Cadillac. At one point, she even set up a pied-à-terre—or stab pad, as we say in Youngstown—with another married Packard Electric man, who left her one day amid candlelight and takeout food, never to return. From that point on, whether Mom was coping at home with Les and Jeffrey, or grinding out a shift at the plant, or floating about Youngstown in her pink suit, she relied heavily on Valium, which was freely dispensed by North Side Hospital's head of psychiatrics—in exchange for what, I can only guess.

Home and religion also went hand-in-hand. I went with Mom to Shannon Road to listen to an Evangelical preacher named Reverend Hewison, a slick, handsome snake oil salesman who excelled not so much at saving souls as at raising money.

After a while, I quit for good and for good reasons: 1. A young handicapped man was banned for overly loud clapping during hymnal songs, and 2. The Good Reverend shot a neighbor's cat because it had strayed into his yard.

Billy became a surrogate big brother to Jeffrey, who was becoming intensely interested in music. Jeffrey drove an expensive white Trans Am around town, played in the marching band, took piano lessons, went to Paris on a school trip, and generally lived the life of a privileged orphan. He adored Billy, who stood proudly as Jeffrey pulled off an amazing piano recital that touched the Stambaugh Auditorium audience at his high school graduation.

Aunt Ginny and Uncle Chuck finally married in 1978. With the years of sneaking around mostly behind them, Gigi and Chuck became officially the life of the party. Ginny worked in the transportation office at Packard Electric, and Uncle Chuck worked in the offices at the railroad and also served as head of the credit union. They golfed, gambled, and spoiled their kids rotten. Both Ginny and Chuck made good livings, with extra income from rental properties they'd purchased and fixed up. Chuck's boys were the same age as Ginny's daughter, Heather, and weekend fun was built around the kids: birthdays, sporting events, travel. I loved being a part of it, and Billy did as well, which made me start to think about starting my own family. Only later, when Chuck fell into depression over the unwanted decision for his kids to move to Florida with their mother, did our proximity to my cherished aunt and her magnificent new husband offer anything but delight.

Dad would eventually marry again (and then again), but he was single during these early years when I was with Billy. I saw very little of him, almost like he was one of those old classmates who slowly drifts out of your life. One night, while I was out at The Living Room with Billy, I literally bumped into Dad on the dance floor. He was shimmying and shaking with some young club hopper, and as I turned to see my 50-something-year-old father acting my age, I instantly turned red. Once the song ended, I politely took Dad aside and shared my shock and embarrassment, and that was that—he weaved his way out of the bar and my life, at least for a while.

Les started making serious money building bridges and working in the steel mill, which, among other problems, made him unsuitable to the single dad role thrust upon him during those intervals when Mom disappeared. Some nights, Les would come home black from soot, white rings around his eyes. Other evenings, he would lay on the floor, spent, his knees aching from crawling on construction beams.

Billy and I never talked of marriage. It seemed that the day-to-day overwhelmed any sense of the future, any planning, and Billy and I joined as a team mostly when we had to confront an unpaid bill or shortfall. Even then, more likely than not, we'd procrastinate, mess around, and then bang around, imploring each other to keep it down so the Barrs would not hear what was going on up there.

I got the feeling that, for Billy, this was all as it should be. He'd continue to work a job he hated to keep the peace and pay the bills, all the while looking for opportunities to get back to the bars, to insinuate his way into a road trip, to have his home base with me but freedom in the tingly night air.

One night, two years into this, I was down. I was good at work, loved my colleagues, but on that particular day, I'd made a careless error—not all that damaging, but inconvenient enough that I felt I'd let the office down. I was an excellent student, but that day I'd gotten some negative feedback from a professor and took it personally. I came home to an empty apartment. Billy was out at a fellow musician's gig at Jacob's Club at the edge of town, where you had to check your guns as you paid the cover fee. I was home alone, or home with Lovie, who fixed his sad eyes on my sad eyes. The apartment was a mess, and I, being a meticulous and tidy person, could not even flop down and decompress without straightening up. Billy's clothes littered the floor. I lifted up his shirt and sniffed it—perfume. I grabbed his jeans and inhaled—perfume. I lifted his underwear and smelled—perfume.

Once I had it in my head, I could smell perfume everywhere, though I reminded myself, and finally convinced myself, it was probably just me: my scent, all of it. They were just dirty clothes, after all: who knew?

As I straightened the apartment, I came across my old address book. It was a pink padded book, thick, that at one time doubled as my hope chest. In that pink padded book, I recorded not only numbers and addresses, but also goals and wishes and dreams—all of them, I saw now as I thumbed through, dead. Dallas Cowboys cheerleader: dead. Fordham University: dead. Playboy Bunny: dead. There were phone numbers to the admission offices of Oral Roberts University, Bowling Green University, and YSU. The name of Barbizon School of Modeling's director. There were scrawls and swirls and hearts (some with arrows shot through) in both black and pink ink. Addresses of summer jobs I've had through the years; pageant owners who I often helped out; my baton teacher from Ravenna.

*Frankie Valli's Wife.*

There, in the margin of that notation, was a number: Frankie's manager, Brian Avnet. I dialed. It rang. He answered. I left a message. When Frankie called back, saying, "I'd love to see you again," he rattled off a list of places where he'd be appearing.

I chose Chicago.

Frankie said, "Great, April. Brian will set it up. The plane ticket will be at the airport when you get there."

*Modeling portfolio.*

# THE SAME OLD SONG?

The nearest airport was in Vienna, very close to Liberty Township, where I spent all of those years being my best. I needed a ride, and I needed a dog-sitter for Lovie, and maybe for those reasons, or maybe because some anxiety or giddiness made me want to blurt out, I told Mom my plans. She disapproved.

I sipped tea, swinging my feet back and forth in my old bedroom, the white canopy bed and assorted childhood treasures strewn about, but the décor strangely altered, the walls and furniture and lighting and carpet changed to a brownish-pink theme, like a raging paintbrush had set out to obscure my formative years. We pointed and counter-pointed. I looked out of the picture window, trying to see the world again through innocent eyes. I spotted my worn and neglected Frankie albums and the silly Frankie hat.

"It's something I have to do," I proclaimed.

"Poor Billy," Mom sighed.

"I'm single," I said.

Mom disagreed. She gave me the ride anyway. At the airport, I spun toward the ticket counter, like Dorothy swirling out of Kansas with no apparent way home.

The ticket was there, and good thing: we didn't have much money, and what little we did have was impossible for me to hide. As I rushed to my gate, I realized Frankie was a man of his word. I trusted him. He did not promise much, but he made good on the few promises he did make. I imagined Billy coming home to an empty apartment, looking for me, looking for a note, looking for anything that would tell him where I was. I'd decided against lying because I was so bad at it. I'd decided against the truth because it was so repulsive. But I knew that when Billy discovered Lovie was gone, he'd know I was gone, too. I'd convinced myself that I needed out, that I deserved out, and that Billy would only need about thirty seconds to find my replacement. I was going to Chicago.

Funny thing about concert hopping was: I never really experienced the cities. In my imagination, concert locales were part of the allure, part of the charms and energy of cosmopolitan cities like New York, San Francisco, Washington, DC, Dallas, and Atlanta.

In Chicago, there were no plans to see the Sears Tower, or take a twirl on Navy Pier's Ferris Wheel, or visit the cultural institutions like the Shedd Aquarium and the Field Museum, or romp through the great Grant Park, or sun on the spectacular Oak Street Beach. No. The plan was, simply, to meet Frankie. To watch Frankie perform. To screw Frankie. Repeat.

I suppose I so desperately wanted my affair with a rock star to be, well, like an affair with a rock star, that I tried to make the story I told myself fit the story I wanted to hear. I told myself it was glamorous. Exciting. Impressive. And it was just enough of those things to maintain my self-delusion, but not enough to make me happy. What I wanted, really, was what I had always wanted, something simple and yet elusive: love.

Brian picked me up at O'Hare Airport and drove me to the Palmer House, where he took my luggage up and told me that Frankie would be back when he finished sound check. I got comfortable. I changed from my travel clothes, a simple pair of jeans, brown suede boots, and a tweed blazer, into a long, fitted gypsy dress in muted soft green corduroy with running on the waist and an ankle flared skirt. I lay back on the feather and down pillows. This was now *everything*. In my mind, I had left Billy—not Going Away For The Weekend left, but Gone For Good. I was tossing aside the slow-churning domestic life—the life of a start-up girlfriend doing start-up academic work while holding down a start-up job—and gambling on the chance to be fully alive, fully invested, already *arrived*.

I waited, laying there on the pristine, white, 800-thread count Egyptian cotton sheets for 30 minutes, 60 minutes, my soft skin tickling the soft linen, excited to see Frankie again, but thinking, too, about my life. Who was I? Who did I want to be? How was I going to get there? I kept circling back to these same questions and wondering if I would ever have answers, insisting I get them *now*. I was confused and lonely. I wanted a hero to rescue me, and the longer I lay there, the more I knew Frankie was that hero.

He arrived. It was the same Frankie who'd signed my program as a five-year-old girl; the Frankie who'd advised me to stay pretty and do my studies; the Frankie who'd taken my virginity; the Frankie who'd urged me to go to college; the Frankie of the stage; the Frankie of the screen; the Frankie of the bus and my boudoir. Blonde highlights peaked out through brown dye at Frankie's temples, wrinkles spread out from his eyes, and there was a slight sag to his shoulders. His forehead appeared unusually taut for a man his age, which, by then, was around 47. But he was fit, tan, and immaculately dressed, and there was still a sparkle to his bluish-green cow eyes. As he appraised me, laying there in wait, I appraised him. God, I loved Frankie. He was the master and I was the slave, and I was unequipped to identify this feeling as a psychological impairment. I just wanted that feeling he gave me, a feeling I'd not found with anyone else.

Frankie started to unbutton his custom-made Italian shirt, and then slowly stripped away the rest of his clothes before strutting, naked, for my viewing pleasure. I wondered if Frankie's peacock act came naturally or if it had developed as he grew into a star. This time, Frankie need not instruct me on the *whats* and *wheres* and *hows*. I was all grown up: a beautiful, sexy *woman*. No longer a silly girl. I wanted to show him that I was not the innocent, naïve April whom he could put on the shelf when he was done. For starters, I planned to make love to him like it was the Olympic Gold Medal round of sexual intercourse. Frankie didn't need to tell me to undress, turn over, or moan. I kissed him: long and hard and deep, watched his eyes roll back, his body fall into a trance. I grabbed him like an animal, taking what I wanted. I touched him, tickled him, teased him, and guided his hand to where I wanted to be touched, tickled, and teased. I endeavored not merely to please him, but to release in him every emotion stored up during the course of our long sabbatical. I wanted him to feel the pent-up emotions coursing through me, and I wanted him to beg me to swallow him whole. We did it up and down, back and forth, over and sideways, until I felt dizzy— drunk, almost—from being joined, literally and figuratively.

Then it was over. I came, he came, we all came, and as always, the wet spots on the sheet represented more than sperm and sweat for me—they formed an intense chemical compound of which the key ingredient was love. We lay there, entangled, panting. I noodled against him and stroked his earlobe with the back of my fingers. Then Frankie said, "Did you know kids can get scholarships for golfing?"

I stopped stroking Frankie's ear. I had almost forgotten how we'd pick up in the middle of conversations we'd never had, conversations about Frankie having a wife, or Frankie having children, or Frankie getting divorced, or Frankie getting married again.

Somehow Frankie assumed I knew all about his private life, even though he never, ever discussed it. Maybe this was the narcissist in him. Maybe he assumed I and every other person on Earth knew all about the Great Frankie Valli: his trials, his tribulations, his triumphs. And I guess I did. I knew about Mary Ann, I knew that he thought she was crazy, and that she was as good as gone. I knew about his new girlfriend. I knew that he had children. I don't know how I knew, since all I read were concert reviews, billboard statistics, and fluff pieces. The era of pop culture fascination and especially media intrusion was still a fledgling industry back then.

"Of course," I said. "There are scholarships available for just about everything: sports, music, science…" I trailed off. Frankie, I felt, had hijacked our special moment. He was not thinking about me or about love, he was thinking of bills, of his kids—of his life without me. I was angry. I was sad. I was desperate. "I mean these kids—I know these kids," Frankie continued. "Great golfers. And now they're going to college for free."

Frankie said this as though it were a revelation, though to me it seemed common knowledge. I grew silent, more an observer than a participant in our discussion. As I listened, Frankie made this and that statement, some of it just plain wrong. I knew not to argue. Frankie became cranky and angry when anybody contradicted him, though the more he talked, the more emboldened I felt. Frankie always played the role of the wise adult, the protective father, but I now sensed this was no longer valid. Maybe it was the simple fact that I'd been to college and he hadn't, or that I engaged with books and current events and he didn't.

He said, "I know you're a good girl, April, I know that. But don't ever do drugs, ever! It'll be nothing but trouble, believe me."

I didn't know this at the time, but earlier that year, 1980, Frankie's stepdaughter Celia had died in a car wreck. Later his daughter Francine died of a drug overdose. This was part of Frankie's other—*real?*—life that he never shared. I took it as more small talk, like when Frankie ragged about new music and how electronics were replacing musicians; or like when he advised me to be a big fish in a small pond. But I was in no mood for small talk.

"So what happens after Chicago?" I asked.

"I'd have to check," Frankie said. "Florida, I remember."

"With us, I mean."

Frankie got out of bed, silent, and grabbed the remote control. He punched the on button and clicked from one to another channel. "Did you see *Grease*?" he asked.

I told him it was fabulous, but sensed that, like the TV, he was switching me to another channel. One hour into a two-day visit and already I felt uneasy. Frankie clearly thought of this as frivolous, just fun, and I struggled to imagine how I could get him to reconfigure our relationship as permanent, serious. Frankly, I was not up to the task. Heroes should not have to be coerced to rescue. They just do it, out of love, out of gallantry, with courage, with humility.

The next two days were a whirlwind. Press parties, sound checks, meet-and-greets. Limos whisking us here and there. The concerts at the Arie Crown Theater were lovely, but as I watched from the wings, I was nostalgic, almost like one of those moments when you know, even as it's happening, that you'll want to travel back, if only in your head. Frankie now played "Grease" at the concert, as well as "December, 1963 (Oh, What A Night)" and other hits from the past five, six, seven years. As I listened to his songbook, I realized it encompassed nearly two decades—and that I, though not yet 23—had been a part of his life for nearly that long.

Outside the concert hall, fans asked for my autograph, and

me, old hand at it now, replied, "Who is this for?" I'd ask in a sweet voice, but my resentment toward Frankie seethed. I wanted satisfaction. I wanted closure. I wanted revenge.

We shuffled back and forth between the hotel and the concert venue, sprinkled with occasional forays to dining spots. The so-called partying mostly took place in the Green Room or the hotel bar. Each time we made love seemed more and more routine, as if for Frankie it was on par with warming his vocal cords or getting a good night's sleep. Our pillow talk, too, grew routine, and during these intimate chats, I began to detect notes of the blue-collar New Jersey boy, cutting hair and dreaming big. Whenever I mentioned my job or college, Frankie offered support but was always quick to change the subject. Frankie responded with non-sequiturs to my rambles about, say, an eligibility case, with something like, "Did you see they got a news station, it's all day and night, every day, never stops?" Was Frankie anti-intellectual, or just clinging to his roots? Did he resent that his pretty little play-thing had a brain? Was I becoming one of those intellectual elites so many people from my hometown detested? Or was it just that my mind was catching up to my body, and that Frankie cared more about the former than the latter?

The Four Seasons were all new, much younger than the Four Seasons whom they'd replaced. The idea, I guess, was that Frankie could age all he wanted, but the backup crew had to get with the moment. Something else had changed, namely that the young Seasons did not seem to revere or respect or fear Frankie in the same way as their older counterparts. These were musicians roughly my age, and when we talked, it was no longer a little girl-toy making small talk with the grown-ups. We were laughing, having fun, flirting, and Frankie did not like it. We were at a group dinner in the meet-and-greet room when the Seasons' new guitarist approached me. He was drunk, and so was I, a little. He started telling me about his home, Las Vegas, telling me about the gorgeous weather, the fantastic hotels and buffets, the music, the gambling, his old neighborhood, the non-stop fun. "You should come out there with me, I'd show you a good time."

I glanced at Frankie. He glared back. His was the face of a man worried not about love but about material possessions, of which, I suppose, I counted as one, a red Ferrari about to be repossessed. I shrugged. I still wanted Frankie—that would not change for many years, and maybe, in retrospect, it was not all my fault. My child and young adult and fully mature psyches were all jumbled, and I wondered then, and still wonder now, what would have happened if we had waited. I thought of myself at 16 as fully responsible for my actions, but many years later, when I watched my own daughter enter puberty, so fragile, so vulnerable, I would have called the cops on some old man making advances, rock star or not.

So here was an offer, and what the hell? Maybe this would make Frankie jealous, or maybe it would just be an adventure, nothing more, or maybe we'd really like each other. Would this make me a groupie? Would this lead to a life as a hanger-on? I'd tried, without success, to plot out my future; maybe it was time to takes things as they came. Not every question has an answer.

We crawled inside the long, black stretch limo, out of the crisp November air, the brilliant Chicago skyline on the horizon. Frankie and I were seated side by side, a couple, for now. We weren't even really friends, more a man and a woman inhabiting the same space inside a fantasy. When the time came, I would be gone and all trace of me wiped out. For the first time, I tried to look, really look, at my surroundings: all this luxury, the gorgeous city, the fine food and drink, the talented companions. I looked from one to another skyscraper and thought, "Each one of those buildings must have a story." I didn't know any of them, but I vowed that, from now on, I would listen for them. I was an emotional wreck, but I needed to understand all the ways in which I was fortunate, blessed beyond what most anybody could expect.

I stared out the windows and up at the stars and moon, hazy celestial blotches competing with the bright artificial downtown lights. Suddenly, a beat-up red Nova pulled beside our limo, and out jumped this lanky, beautiful, harrowed young man, his curly hair flying, his blue eyes steaming. He looked, despite his clear anger, incapable of harming an ant.

Billy walked up to the limo at a steady pace—left, right, left, right. I froze. With each step, I felt my world shaking, trembling, that much closer to calamity. "Jesus!" I thought. "How did Billy even…?" Then I remembered: I'd told Mom, and Mom of course told Billy. Frankie ordered the driver to stop. Frankie shot me a "What the hell is this?" look and lowered the electric window halfway. "You have my wife!" Billy exclaimed. "I want my wife back. Now!"

I looked from Billy to Frankie, Frankie to Billy. For once, my choice was black and white: this or that, now or never. I felt a surge of power. My choice, my life, my decision. Billy or Frankie. Frankie or Billy.

"Is that true?" Frankie asked.

"We're not married," I said, but my eyes hinted that there was more to the story. Billy and I meant something to each other, in ways that Frankie and I did not. We were finding our way in the world. Maybe we'd find it together, maybe we'd find it apart, but for now, anyway, we cared and loved one another, and all the problems we'd had, all the problems to come, could not undermine our sincerity.

Frankie looked at my ring finger. There was just finger. "We live together," I explained. Billy looked broken, bent, distraught. "I better go home."

Frankie nodded. Like a father, he knew what was right, even when it was hard. I tried to hug Frankie—I sensed this was our good-bye—but he shied away. No kiss. No nothing. My luggage would be delivered to my home, per Brian, who was in the front of the limo taking orders. *Your fantasy has now concluded; please head to the exit in an orderly fashion.*

Then it was just Billy and I and a lot of sorting out to do. At first, I was just angry, pure and simple, and on the tense ride back to Youngstown, I thought only of all the ways Billy had done me wrong. The anger spread to Mom—what betrayal!—and to Aunt Ginny—she could have stopped this!—and then the intensity of the anger bled out, leaving me just tired and weary. Billy had been gallant. He had been decisive. He had been willing to fight for me, and in this moment, he felt his world was lost without me. I considered the contrast between Billy and Frankie, two men from entirely different generations. Billy had guts and heart, and he wanted us to belong to each other. Frankie had money and fame, and there was really no *us* about it. Eventually, the air softened, and I learned that Billy had driven in a desperate race, on no sleep, through the black of night, and as I listened to him describe his fear and loneliness and sense of betrayal, I thought about those Hollywood endings in which the frantic lover wildly, and against all odds, races to the airport just in time to save a romance that clearly, to everybody else, is destined to work. I *did* love Billy.

Frankie called the next day and, in his best Father Knows Best voice, told me, "You should stay with Bill. Work it out."

It was November of 1980, and Ronald Regan had just defeated Jimmy Carter to become our new president. Earlier in the year, CNN had launched the first round-the-clock news station; soon, John Lennon would be assassinated. Change was constant, and I was trying to become the kind of person who adapted to it rather than tried to stop it. Soon after the calendar changed again, on the first day of spring, 1981, Billy and I would marry.

I'd love to be able to say that this was the end of Frankie, that I did not go to Vegas to meet the guitarist, that I never looked back, and that Billy and I lived happily ever after. I'd like to say that the proposal was sweet and the wedding was spectacular, and that Billy, from that moment on, refused to be with any woman but me. I'd like to say that it was all laughter and no tears, that I learned, right then and there, to be content, to be determined, to be open and honest, to confront my emotional troubles head on. But none of that is true, exactly.

What is true is that Billy and I decided to give ourselves a chance, and for the next two decades, almost, I fought to make both our lives happy, and eventually to make the lives of my daughter and son happy. What is true is that I *was* happy, much of the time, and that I found happiness within myself rather than in the leftover bright lights of a pop star. I found happiness in my career, in lifelong learning, in being a good mother, in small moments like when Billy and I watched the morning news together or rocked to the Lake Erie waves on his grandparents' little boat. Sometimes, sure, I found happiness in a pair of Prada shoes or a Burberry handbag. But I learned that those things were just accessories.

The part of myself I gave up when I gave up Frankie was damaged, and in retrospect, it had been since the beginning. I gave up my subservient nature, the instinct to be acted upon rather than to act. I tried mightily to change my outlook on men and to reconfigure my definition of a meaningful life. More than anything, I took inventory of what I had rather than what I lacked. It took time—addicts like me never really recover—and during moments of insecurity or loneliness or self-loathing, my thoughts would turn to Frankie. *What if? Is it too late? Why can't I still be April The Shining Light?*

For a while, I blamed Frankie, Mom, everyone, believing that they'd been wrecking balls and I a demolition project. But my life was not a wreck—not perfect but surely purposeful. I was a wife and a mom; I had a thriving career; I had friends and family who loved me. At some point, I knew that what I had inherited I now owned, and while I inherited a good deal of misery, I also inherited an abundance of joy.

I knew things were better, I knew I was healing, when one day, years removed from Frankie, cradling Dana in my arms while little Grant bounced about, Lovie licking my toes, I heard, "My Eyes Adore You," and thought not, "What is Frankie doing?" or, "Is Frankie thinking of me?" or "Could it still work?" I thought, only, "That's nice; I love that song." And sang along.

*Backstage sticker from a Chicago Theatre concert.*

*April and Frankie, three decades after that first concert.*